Outreach Skits for Youth Ministry

Loveland, Colorado

Note

The price of this text includes the right for you to make as many copies of the skits as you need for your immediate youth group. If another church or organization wants copies of these skits, it must purchase *Outreach Skits for Youth Ministry* in order to receive performance rights.

Outreach Skits for Youth Ministry

Copyright © 1999 Group Publishing, Inc.

Credits
Contributing Authors: Melody DeLeon, Julianne Bruce, James D. Freeman, Teresa McCasland
Acquisitions Editor: Amy Simpson
Editor: Dennis R. McLaughlin
Creative Development Editor: Dave Thornton
Chief Creative Officer: Joani Schultz
Copy Editor: Betty Taylor
Art Director: Kari K. Monson
Computer Graphic Artist: Desktop Miracles
Cover Designer: Becky Hawley
Production Manager: Peggy Naylor

Unless otherwise noted, Scripture taken from the HOLY BIBLE, NEW INTERNATIONAL VERSION®. Copyright © 1973, 1978, 1984 by International Bible Society. Used by permission of Zondervan Publishing House. All rights reserved.

Library of Congress Cataloging-in-Publication Data
Outreach skits for youth ministry.
     p.   cm.
    Includes index.
    ISBN 0-7644-2100-X (alk. paper)
    1. Drama in Christian education. 2. Church group work with youth.
 I. Group Publishing.
 BV1534.4.098   1999
 246'.72--dc21

98-39392
CIP

10 9 8 7 6 5 4 3 2   08 07 06 05 04 03 02 01 00

Printed in the United States of America.
Visit our Web site: www.grouppublishing.com

Contents

Help From Above

Introduction

Have you ever been fishing? OK! So that's not the first question you expected to be asked after opening a book of youth skits. But you'll have to admit, there are a lot of youth skit-books out there you have to fish in for awhile before you find something relating to the lives of teenagers. Well, not with *Outreach Skits for Youth Ministry.*

All twenty-four skits speak directly to the real issues today's teenagers face every day. The four contributing authors have crafted each skit to be amazingly thought provoking and challenging.

In addition, these skits were specifically written to be "seeker sensitive." You will be surprised at how each one introduces the Christian message without alienating those who have a limited understanding of Christianity, or who have no experience with God's Word at all. A few skits even have evangelistic messages and can be used in direct outreach situations.

You'll quickly discover that each skit is easy to perform and no more than fifteen minutes long. Because of their flexibility, they can be performed in a variety of settings, including worship services, special services, informal settings, and outreach events.

As if the skits by themselves are not thought provoking enough, each one is followed by a discussion activity. The discussion activities challenge teenagers to think deeply about faith issues and encourage them to make direct application as well.

For easy use, the skits are divided into three sections: **"Relationships Along the Way," "Obstacles in the Path,"** and **"Help From Above."**

Relationships Along the Way

Who wouldn't agree that life is all about our "Relationships Along the Way"?

You'll want to be sure to blast off in a space shuttle with the first four teenagers to visit the moon. Watch as they struggle with how they will get along together in such a small space colony in *Found in Space.*

Or agonize with Josh as he is forced to make a choice. Will he choose to spray paint graffiti on a wall to gain the respect of two uncool guys, or will he learn the meaning of true friendship in *In the Name of Friendship.*

You may also choose from one of six other skits about relationships that involve friends and family.

Obstacles in the Path

Not much in life is more frustrating than those irritating "Obstacles in the Path."

You will definitely sense a bit of ironic humor as you become acquainted with Mr. Hipp. No one needs to convict him of being a hypocrite—he does a sufficient job of it himself in *The Tale of Mr. Hipp.*

You'll also probably recognize Mrs. Thornberry. She is more concerned about Joel wearing his blue jeans to church than she is with him as a person. But watch as Lizzy tries to defend him in *Not the Place for Me.*

You'll definitely empathize with Casey as her alcoholic parents embarrass her in front of her friends in *Nobody's Supposed to Know.*

Or you may choose from among seven other skits that speak very significantly about the problems teenagers face every day.

Help From Above

Don't give up yet! Even in the midst of daily trials, there is always "Help From Above."

You will undoubtedly want to climb the tree with the Z man to see if you can catch a glimpse of what he sees in *The Z Tree.*

Or have you ever wanted a date with a guy named *Moonbeam?* If so, you need to meet Beth. After her "heavenly" experience, she'll probably be willing to give him up—or is it too late? You decide in *Will the Real Christian Please Step Up.*

Go behind the scenes and compete on the "Bull's-Eye Dating Game Show" for a date with a surfer dude named Bob. Of course, Bob's not sure whether Einstein or God created the universe—but no one can deny that he's one cool surfer dude in *Bull's-Eye.*

You may also choose from among three other skits that will definitely remind you that God is in charge!

Whatever skit you begin with, be sure to sit back in your seat. And I do mean sit back! Even buckle up if you can! Because all twenty-four skits promise to take you, and your teenagers, right to the edge. But leave your fishing pole at home. You won't need it!

Relationships Along the Way

❧

Found in Space

Scripture: 1 Corinthians 13

Topic: Relationships

Setting: The first four teenagers to visit the moon are traveling in a space shuttle. The set consists of four chairs placed closely together in two rows, similar to seats on a bus or an airplane.

Props: The Attendant needs a tray with three small packages of juice and several small bags of peanuts.

Characters:
Buddy—a teenage guy
Priscilla—a teenage girl
John—a teenage guy
Amanda—a teenage girl
Attendant—a male or female flight attendant

◆◆◆ Script ◆◆◆
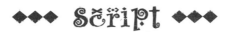

Buddy: Wow! We are the first high school students to visit the new moon colony. I can't believe we're actually in the shuttle and on the way to spend three months up there.

Priscilla: We've trained long enough. It's about time we got to make the trip.

John: Yeah, really.

Amanda: Look! Out the window! *(Points stage left.)* You can see North America! Isn't this great?

Buddy: Yeah, but I'll have to admit that I'm a little nervous.

Priscilla: I know. Have you seen the list of instructions for the bathroom on this thing? When they say that space travel is an adventure, they're not kidding!

Buddy: Oh, that's not what bothers me; it's how crowded it's going to be.

Priscilla: What do you mean by crowded?

Buddy: There's not a whole lot of room at the moon base, and I'm concerned about how well we'll get along with each other while we're there. Don't get me wrong. I come from a large family, so I'm used to having to share a room.

Amanda: Sounds like you'll do fine.

Buddy: I hope so; otherwise this will be a long three months.

John: Yeah, really!

Priscilla: I don't think crowding will be a problem.

Amanda: Aren't you an only child, Priscilla?

Priscilla: Yes.

Amanda: Well, aren't you concerned about how you'll handle living with lots of people in a confined area?

Priscilla: Not at all. If the rest of you will just stay out of my way, we'll all do fine.

Buddy: *(To Priscilla)* If *we* stay out of *your* way?

Priscilla: Sure. That's not too much to ask, is it?

(Buddy, Amanda, and John all look at one another with surprise.)

Buddy: Uh, nothing personal! But staying out of the way is not an option. *(To Priscilla)* I think you're the one who will have to cope with things.

Priscilla: *(Starts to get angry.)* I beg your pardon!

Amanda: *(Quickly)* You know, guys, there may be a better way to deal with this. In my family we say that good relationships are built on love.

Buddy: You mean like boyfriends and girlfriends?

Amanda: I mean any way that people relate to each other. A relationship is like a living thing. To be healthy it needs to be cared for, and love is the basic ingredient for getting along.

Buddy: What does this have to do with being crowded?

Amanda: When we get to the moon, we'll need to work hard so that we don't get on each other's nerves, and love is an important part of getting along.

Buddy: But it isn't always easy to show love, even with friends and family members.

John: Yeah, really!

Amanda: Love takes a lot of practice.

Priscilla: You make love sound like a musical instrument.

Amanda: In some ways they're similar. The more you work at it, the more it becomes a part of who you are.

Attendant: *(Enters, walking slowly as if in zero gravity.)* May I get you anything to drink?

Priscilla: Wow, I didn't know there were flight attendants on the space shuttle.

Attendant: Oh yes, we've come a long way since the nineties.

Amanda: I'll have a soft drink.

John: Yeah, me too.

Priscilla: Orange juice, please.

Buddy: Do you have any peanuts?

Attendant: Yes, we do. I'll be right back. *(Exits.)*

Buddy: So what are some of the things that we'll need to do to practice love?

Amanda: The best description of love I know comes from the Bible. In 1 Corinthians it says that love is patient and kind, that it does not envy or boast, it's not proud or rude or self-seeking. It's not easily angered. There's more, but that's the gist of it.

Priscilla: That's a lot to keep track of.

Buddy: I can see why it takes practice.

John: Yeah, really!

Buddy: *(Points stage right.)* Hey, look over there. Isn't that Mars in the distance?

Priscilla: *(Looks where Buddy is pointing.)* It sure looks different when you're out of the atmosphere. *(To Amanda)* So how is it that love will make things better for us on the moon?

Amanda: Life is full of relationships. Some are very important, like who you date and the members of your family. Some are less important, like the checker in the supermarket who you see for only five minutes a week.

Buddy: We won't be seeing any supermarket checkers for a while.

John: Yeah, really!

Amanda: That's true. But there will be other types of people. If a relationship is motivated by envy or mistrust or greed, then any problems will be hard to overcome. But if the relationship is based on acceptance, trust, and concern for others, then problems will be less difficult to deal with. Jesus himself wanted people to love God first and then to love and care for each other.

Attendant: *(Enters holding tray with two juice packages and several bags of peanuts. Attendant hands the drinks to Amanda and John and the peanuts to Buddy.)* Here you are. *(To Priscilla)* I'm sorry. I can't seem to find any orange juice. Would apple juice be OK?

Priscilla: *(Becomes angry.)* What kind of a lousy shuttle is this? *(Points to Buddy.)* He got his peanuts. I want my orange juice.

Attendant: *(Perplexed)* I'm terribly sorry. I'm doing the best I can.

Priscilla: Try harder! Keep looking!

Attendant: I'll be right back. *(Exits.)*

Priscilla: *(Yells after Attendant.)* And don't come back 'til you find my *orange juice.*

Buddy: Hey, there's a relationship—Priscilla and the flight attendant. *(To Amanda)* How does love work here?

Amanda: A relationship built on love realizes that it's not the attendant's fault there's no orange juice and trusts the attendant is trying to help you. While a relationship built on anger would not give the attendant a chance.

Priscilla: *(Becomes defensive.)* Look, I just wanted something to drink. *(Begins to look at John's soft drink. She's up to something.)* Hey, John, did I ever tell you how much I admire your attitude?

John: *(Looks nervous.)* Really?

Priscilla: *(Still talking to John)* I sure am getting thirsty. You know, if you're not going to drink that cola…

Amanda: Priscilla! That's John's drink. You should be ashamed of yourself.

John: Yeah, really!

Amanda: Trying to manipulate or take advantage of someone else is not acting out of love. *(To John)* God wants what is best for us, John, and that doesn't include being victims of someone else's envy or selfishness.

(Priscilla crosses her arms and looks the other way. John doesn't say anything but stares back at Amanda.)

Amanda: John, you don't seem to ever say much.

John: Really?

Amanda: And I've got to tell you, it's about to drive me nuts. *(Getting a little angry)* How come you never talk?

John: *(Looks at Amanda with a long pause.)* What would you like me to say?

Amanda: Anything! Express an opinion. Make a comment. Just quit saying "yeah, really!"

Priscilla: *(To Amanda)* Excuse me, but are you really practicing love here?

Amanda: What do you mean?

Priscilla: John's shy.

John: Yeah, really!

(Amanda shoots a glare at John, who quickly looks away.)

Priscilla: But you're trying to make him talk and be more, well, more like you. It seems to me that you should accept John for who he is and not try to change him. Am I right?

Buddy: She's got a point. That's what we try to do around my house, all twelve of us.

Amanda: *(Realizes she's been wrong.)* Yes, Priscilla does have a point. *(To John)* I'm sorry, John. I shouldn't have said what I did. There's nothing wrong with who you are.

Attendant: *(Enters.)* I'm sorry. There seems to have been a mix-up. All the orange juice has been sent up to first class.

Priscilla: First class! On the space shuttle?

Attendant: Oh, yes. We've come a long way since the nineties. *(To Priscilla)* I'll keep trying to get your drink. And again, I'm sorry.

Priscilla: *(Looks at the others for a moment, and then to the Attendant.)* That's OK. Just do your best.

Attendant: Thank you. *(Exits.)*

Buddy: Well, I think we've all learned something on this flight.

John: Yeah, really!

(He and the others look at one another and laugh.)

John: Look! *(Points stage left.)* Over there! It's the moon. We're almost there.

Priscilla: Wow! The moon! I can't believe it.

◆◆◆ Discussion Activity ◆◆◆

On a large sheet of newsprint write the word "relationships." Begin by asking the group members to name as many types of relationships as they can think of. As they list them, record their responses on the newsprint. *(These might include relationships between parents and children, employees and bosses, brothers and sisters, friends, and so forth.)*

Read 1 Corinthians 13 aloud to the group, and ask:

● **According to the passage, what are the things that love *does not do?*** (Write the responses on another sheet of newsprint.)

● **According to the passage, what are the things that love *does*?** (Write these on newsprint as well.)

Pick one or two of the relationship types from the first list. Ask the group to discuss how the things love *does not do* might affect each relationship. Then discuss how the things love *does* would affect each relationship.

Ask group members to think about examples from the skit, and then ask the following questions:

● **Name some examples from the skit of things that love *does not do*.**

● **What examples were there of things that love *does*?**

● **How might we define a healthy relationship?**

Jack and the Paycheck

Scripture: Matthew 5:13-16

Topic: Generosity

Setting: Two teens, Jack and Maggie, are walking to the mall from their home. The other characters encounter Jack and Maggie at intervals across the stage.

Props: A chair on one side of the stage represents Maggie's home. You will also need a book for Maggie to read, a paycheck for Jack, and a hammer or toolbox for Randy. The Bell Ringer needs a large pot or bucket, a small bell, and a sign that reads "Help for a Hungry World."

Characters:
Maggie—a teenage girl
Jack—Maggie's younger brother, also a teenager
Randy—a friend of Jack and Maggie
Bell Ringer—a man or woman collecting for charity
Young Man—a young homeless person

◆◆◆ Script ◆◆◆

(Maggie sits in a comfortable chair reading. Jack enters waving a paycheck.)

Jack: *(Excitedly)* Hey! Look what I got today.

Maggie: What is it?

Jack: My first paycheck. I'm rich!

Maggie: I wouldn't get so worked up about it if I were you.

Jack: *(Ignores her.)* Oh yes! Eighty-seven dollars and nineteen cents. *(He kisses the check.)* Not bad for one week.

Maggie: Yeah, yeah, yeah. You're a millionaire.

Jack: Well, it won't be long now. That's for sure.

Maggie: So what are you going to do with your newfound wealth?

Jack: I'm headed to the mall. I want to stock up on CDs and video games. I've got my shopping list ready.

Maggie: Well, it just so happens that I'm going to the mall too.

Jack: You're welcome to come with me. But I warn you, I'm a young man on a shopping mission. I intend to spend!—eighty-seven dollars and nineteen cents to be exact. And the best part is that next week I get to do it all over again.

Maggie: You'll never be a millionaire if you spend all your money as soon as you get it.

Jack: True. But this is just the beginning. I'll put a little back for larger purchases, like a TV, a better CD player, and someday—a car. Maybe I'll even save a little for the future. But for now, the mall is calling my name.

Maggie: Well, let's not keep the mall waiting. *(She puts down her book and stands.)*

(Jack and Maggie begin to walk across the stage. Randy enters.)

Jack: Look, it's Randy. Hey Randy, what's happening?

Randy: Hey Jack, Maggie. What are you doing?

Maggie: Jack has a paycheck burning a hole in his pocket. We're going to the mall to see how far his money stretches.

Jack: *(To Randy)* Yeah, why don't you come with us? You can watch me spend.

Randy: *(Laughs.)* Sounds like fun, but I'm meeting some guys to go work on a house.

Maggie: A house? Are you working for a builder now?

Randy: No, this is volunteer work. We are helping to provide housing to a family that normally couldn't afford it. You guys ought to tag along. There is a lot to do, and it really will make a difference.

Jack: I don't know, Randy. The last thing I hit with a hammer was my thumbnail. I'm not much good with tools.

Maggie: Me neither. Dad won't even let me near his workshop. He says I could hurt someone, especially myself.

Randy: Well, there are other ways to help. The organization that's building the house is always looking for funds to help with supplies. They've built a dozen houses already, and they'd like to build at least fifty more. You wouldn't believe the number of families that need a home to live in. How about sharing some of that paycheck, Jack?

Jack: *(Looks stunned.)* Uh, well...er...uh, let me get back to you on that. Right now I'm a little short for what I need.

Randy: That's cool. They'll always need it. You all have fun shopping, and I'll see you later.

Maggie: See you, Randy.

Jack: So long. See you later.

(Randy exits.)

Maggie: Jack, you *could* give some of your paycheck to help out with that house. It sounds like a really good thing they're doing.

Jack: Hey, they don't really need my money. They'll get what they need from someone else. In the meantime I've got every penny accounted for. There are two new video games I've got to have, not to mention the new CDs.

(Jack and Maggie begin to walk again and encounter a person ringing a bell and standing next to a large bucket. A sign next to the bucket says, "Help for a Hungry World.")

Bell Ringer: *(Rings a bell and talks loudly.)* Excuse me, could you spare some change to help stamp out hunger?

Jack: *(Trying to walk on by)* Sorry, not today.

Maggie: *(Slowing to a stop next to the Bell Ringer)* Sure, here you go. *(She takes a few coins from her pocket and drops them in the bucket.)* I've heard about all the good work this group does around the world.

Bell Ringer: *(To Maggie)* Thank you. Thank you so much. *(To Jack)* Won't you help?

Jack: *(Not happy at being asked)* Who? Me? I'm sorry, I don't think I can. But maybe you could stop with the ringing. You're giving me a headache.

Bell Ringer: *(Stops ringing the bell.)* Sorry. I've gotten to where I don't even hear it. Are you sure you can't contribute just a little? Help for a Hungry World sends food to famine victims, agricultural help to developing nations, and even helps with nutrition classes in this country.

Jack: Uh, well…uh, I don't know. I couldn't give enough to do any good.

Bell Ringer: Every penny counts. It all helps to make life more meaningful for lots of people around the world.

Maggie: Come on, Jack. You can afford to help a little.

Jack: *(Gives Maggie a dirty look.)* Let me get back to you. I'll see what I can do.

Bell Ringer: OK. *(Starts ringing the bell again.)* Give it some thought, and do what you can.

(Jack and Maggie walk on. A young man in worn clothes enters.)

Young Man: *(To Jack)* I was wondering, could you spare a dollar or two for a hamburger? I haven't eaten since early yesterday.

Jack: *(Answers rudely.)* Are you begging?

Maggie: *(Upset)* Jack! That's not a very nice question!

Jack: *(To Maggie)* I'm sorry. I just want to understand, that's all.

Young Man: I'm on my own and a little short of cash right now, that's all. I don't mean to bother you, and if you can't help, that's cool. God bless. *(He exits.)*

Maggie: I think he was homeless. I can't believe what you said.

Jack: He should go to a shelter or a church for help, shouldn't he? I mean, how much help could we give?

Maggie: I'm beginning to wonder, Jack. You know, if everybody was as stingy with their money as you are, there wouldn't *be* any shelters for homeless people. There wouldn't be any help for *anybody*.

Jack: Look, I'm sorry. I guess I never realized there was as much need as there is. Homes for families, food for the hungry, homeless shelters. Is it so bad to want to spend my money on a few CDs and a couple of videos?

Maggie: No, of course not. But I think in the excitement of earning a paycheck, you've forgotten how important it is to share.

Jack: What do you mean?

Maggie: I mean ever since we were little, Dad has taught us to be thoughtful of others. I just think that you and I could be a little more generous, that's all.

Jack: I'll have to admit, CDs don't seem nearly as important now as they did a little while ago. Maybe I need to rethink my priorities.

Maggie: Let's both start thinking about ways we could be more generous with what we have. Instead of three or four CDs, maybe one or two would do. Then we could share our money with others.

Jack: *(Looks thoughtful.)* Maybe so.

Maggie: We wouldn't solve all the problems of the world by ourselves, but at least we could do our part.

Jack: Yeah. You know, I've got a bunch of CDs at home that I've hardly even heard. I think I'll go home and listen to some of those before I buy any new ones. In the meantime, let's go find that bell ringer so I can help feed the world.

Maggie: Good for you. Let's go.

(They exit back toward "home.")

◆◆◆ Discussion Activity ◆◆◆

Divide the teenagers into groups of two or three. Ask the kids in each group to take turns sharing what they would do if they had $1 million.

On a large sheet of easel paper, write the following:

- A Shelter for Abused Women and Children—$50,000
- A Scholarship Fund for Disabled Youth—$25,000
- A Summer Day Camp for Foster Children—$32,000
- Assistance on Utility Bills for the Elderly—$9,000
- Medical Help for Developing Nations—$15,000
- Bibles and Other Resources for Prison Ministry—$7,000

Inform each group that they have been given a budget of $55,000 to divide among as many needs on the list as they can. The only stipulation is that they must give the full amount shown next to whatever needs they choose. After a suitable time, ask the groups to report on how they divided their money.

Read Matthew 5:13-16 aloud and ask:

- **What choices did you make and how did you decide?**
- **Why is it important to be generous with our money?**
- **At what point should you stop giving? 5 percent, 10 percent, 15 percent? Why?**

To conclude, ask whether any of the teenagers participate regularly in volunteer activities. If so, invite them to tell the group about their experiences. Challenge the teenagers to begin talking about how they might help with a local program.

The Dream Show

Scripture: Genesis 29:1-14

Topic: Family

Setting: This drama takes the form of a late-night, call-in radio show. Roberta and Glazier are sitting behind a desk or table. Those calling in by phone may speak from offstage or may stand on a riser behind Roberta and Glazier.

Props: There should be a large microphone on the desk. If the callers appear onstage, they should each hold a telephone. Roberta should be dressed in her pajamas to signify that she is dreaming.

Characters:
   Glazier Trane—the host of a late-night, call-in radio show
   Roberta—a teenage girl who dreams that she is the show's guest
   Sarah—a caller to the show
   Timothy—a caller to the show
   Matthew—a caller to the show
   Mom—Roberta's mother

◆◆◆ Script ◆◆◆

Glazier: Hello to everyone in radio land and welcome to *The Dream Show*. I'm your host, Glazier Trane, coming to you by way of the DS Radio Network. Tonight our guest is a teenager who is having a little trouble sleeping. Please welcome Roberta.

Roberta: *(Nervously)* Uh, hi. I've never been on the radio before.

Glazier: Hey, relax. Just be yourself and you'll do fine. And remember, you're only dreaming.

Roberta: That's easy for you to say.

Glazier: *(Laughs in a phony way.)* Isn't she funny, folks? So tell me, Roberta, what's family life like for you?

Roberta: Family life? You mean my family?

Glazier: Would you rather talk about *my* family?

Roberta: *(Puzzled)* I don't know *your* family.

Glazier: She's quick, folks. *(Phony laugh)* Then we'd better talk about *your* family, Roberta.

Roberta: Oh. Well, I've got an older brother and a younger sister, and of course my mom and dad.

Glazier: Any pets?

Roberta: A collie named Smartie. And we all live in a house in a busy neighborhood.

Glazier: What sort of things does your family do?

Roberta: My brother, sister, and I all go to school, of course. Dad works as an accountant downtown. Mom is a nurse at the hospital. We all participate in church activities and sports, and we all like to swim in the neighborhood pool. We're pretty busy, especially in the summer with jobs, but we try to take time to be together. For instance, supper time is important to us as a family.

Glazier: I see. Well, as you know, Roberta, this is a call-in show, so we're going to open the phone lines now. Our first call tonight is from Sarah. Are you there, Sarah?

Sarah: *(Holding phone)* Hi, Glazier. Hi, Roberta.

Roberta: Hi, Sarah.

Glazier: What's your comment tonight?

Sarah: It's a question, really. You all are talking about families, but are all families supposed to be exactly like Roberta's, three kids, two parents, and a dog?

Glazier: That's an excellent question. Roberta, should all families look like yours?

Roberta: That's something I've been thinking about a lot too. Some of my friends' families are much different from mine. Sometimes their parents are divorced. Sometimes there are lots of kids, and sometimes just one. I know some people who don't have any children at all. Then yesterday at school, I heard some kids talking, and one told the other he came from a lousy family because he lived with an aunt. That really bothered me. I mean, what *is* a family supposed to be like?

Sarah: Could it be that the importance of a family comes from how the family members interact with each other, and how they care and respond to each other? I'm adopted, but I've always felt loved and cared for by my adoptive parents. I would consider mine a good family.

Roberta: That makes sense to me, and I really appreciate you sharing that with me. *(To Glazier)* This may seem silly, but this has worried me a lot lately.

Glazier: Well, that's why we're here.

Roberta: What do you mean?

Glazier: I mean, we're here to deal with the issues that have been on your mind.

Roberta: Oh, I get it. This is something that I've been concerned about, so now I'm dreaming about it.

Glazier: Exactly. Thanks for calling, Sarah.

Sarah: Thank *you. (Hangs up.)*

Glazier: *(Phony laugh)* We have another call now. This one's from Timothy. Go ahead, Timothy.

Timothy: *(Holding phone)* Yeah, thanks! And thanks for having such a great show.

Glazier: You can thank Roberta. It's her dream. Did you have a question this evening?

Timothy: Yeah. My little brother and I can't seem to agree on anything. Sometimes he makes me so mad I could hit him. What should I do?

Glazier: Well, first of all don't ever resort to violence. That won't solve anything. But let's see, how does your family solve disagreements, Roberta?

Roberta: Usually we all sit down around our dining room table and take turns talking about it. We talk about how we feel, what may have caused the problem, and what we can do to resolve it. When the disagreement is among us kids, my parents try to help us deal with it before it becomes a bigger problem.

Glazier: What if your parents are a part of the disagreement?

Roberta: Then they are usually pretty good about listening to our side of things. They will often work to find a compromise. They want us to respect each other's ideas and opinions and try to listen to what the other person is saying.

Glazier: Listening to each other and respecting one another—those are good ideas for any family. Thanks for your call, Timothy.

Timothy: Sure thing. *(Hangs up.)*

Roberta: I feel kind of funny talking about my family to all your listeners.

Glazier: Hey, relax. I doubt many people are tuned in.

Roberta: *(Points to the real audience.)* What about them?

Glazier: Them? Oh, they're all dreaming, too. Let's take our next call from Matthew.

Matthew: *(Holding phone)* Uh, hello?

Glazier: Yes, you're on the air.

Matthew: I want to tell you, this is the dumbest idea for a show that I've ever heard. Families? I mean, really.

Glazier: I'm sorry you feel that way.

Roberta: What's so dumb about it?

Matthew: It's dumb because families are dumb and more trouble than they're worth.

Roberta: Hey, no family is perfect, and sometimes there can be a lot of pain. But no matter who we are, we have to relate to a family somehow. I think that makes families pretty important and definitely worth talking about.

Matthew: You're nuts!

Roberta: *(Angrily)* I am not! You sound just like my brother.

Matthew: See! It's like I said, families are dumb.

Roberta: Look, my brother and I don't always get along, but I love him anyway. So don't be such a jerk! *(To Glazier)* Can I say that on the radio?

Glazier: It's your dream. Say whatever you want. In the meantime we'll say goodbye to Matthew.

(Matthew looks at the phone in his hand as if he has just been cut off.)

Roberta: Oh, he made me mad!

Glazier: There's one in every dream.

Roberta: *(Thinks for a moment.)* Of course Matthew may have some problems he's dealing with in his family. I may have been a little too rough on him, especially if he feels lonely or depressed. If that's the case, I hope he'll find someone to talk to, a counselor at school or a minister. I hope he'll find someone who will listen and offer some help. And I hope I can be more patient the next time.

Glazier: Speaking of which, let's try another call.

Mom: Roberta dear!

Roberta: *(To Glazier)* This sounds like my mother.

Mom: Yes, dear, this is Mom. I just wanted to make sure you didn't oversleep. We have a busy day ahead of us.

Roberta: Is it time to wake up already?

Mom: Almost! So finish up the show, and don't hit the snooze button on your alarm clock.

Roberta: You know about *The Dream Show?*

Mom: I won't in the morning, of course. But right now I do. Listen, dear, one thing you haven't mentioned about families is that they help make us who we are. One way of understanding ourselves is to look at our families.

Roberta: Wow! That's a good point, Mom. A lot of who I am has to do with where I come from.

Mom: That doesn't necessarily mean that you'll be a nurse or an accountant when you're older. But you will carry a lot of your family with you. Just thought I'd throw that in. I'll see you in the kitchen in a few minutes.

Roberta: OK, Mom.

(Mom hangs up.)

Roberta: Well I guess it's about time for me to wake up. Thanks for giving me the chance to think about what it means to be a family.

Glazier: Sure! That's what *The Dream Show* is all about. Join us next time, folks, when our guest will be a man in Alabama who ate a large sausage pizza just before bedtime.

Roberta: That sounds like a nightmare.

Glazier: No joke! Good night, and pleasant dreams.

◆◆◆ Discussion Activity ◆◆◆

In any group of young people, a variety of family "shapes and sizes" will usually be represented. It may be helpful for teenagers to see that families don't all have to be alike.

Invite members of the group to describe their own families. Ask them a few questions such as how many members are in their families, what are family members' ages, and whether or not they have any extended family or special relationships within the household, such as grandparents or foster children.

Ask:

● What are some ways that your families deal with disagreements and other problems?

● What did Roberta discover about what families "look like"?

● What are some ways to improve the relationships within a family?

● What challenge did Timothy face in the skit?

● What are some ways that our families affect us, both now and throughout our lives?

● What other kinds of groups or individuals can serve as families?

Putting It in Perspective

Scripture: Ephesians 6:1-4

Topic: Family

Setting: It's Bible study night at church. Everyone starts together, then the larger group breaks up into smaller groups for discussion.

Props: You'll need chairs for everyone (which can be moved around), paper for a paper airplane, and a Bible for Ilsbeth.

Characters:

Jen—Robert and Carlie's fifteen-year-old daughter. She's stressed because she thinks her parents love her brother more than they love her.

Bob—Robert and Carlie's seventeen-year-old son. He's smart and responsible but tired of being pressured to be perfect.

Ron—Mike's seventeen-year-old son. He's sad because his mother died and he has no relationship with his father. He comes across as bitter because he feels defeated.

Mark—Chris' sixteen-year-old son. He's curious and thoughtful. He tries to understand where other people are coming from, including his dad.

Karen—Ilsbeth's sixteen-year-old daughter. She's lonely and feels that her mother doesn't care. She tries too hard to be upbeat.

Mike—Ron's dad. He's been sad and lonely since his wife died. He's frustrated by his inability to make things work with his son.

Robert—Jen and Bob's dad. He's a nice but insecure person who doesn't look any further than the surface of things.

Carlie—Jen and Bob's mom. She's concerned about others and tries to be helpful, but she's clueless about what's really going on with people.

Ilsbeth—Karen's mom. She's an overburdened single mother who is so focused on meeting her goals for her daughter that she doesn't even notice Karen.

Chris—Mark's dad. He's a nice guy who is willing to work hard to have a good relationship with his son.

Pastor

◆◆◆ Script ◆◆◆

(The whole group sits in two rows of chairs with their backs to the audience. Kids sit with their parent(s), but pay attention to one another—Jen and Bob elbow each other; Mark and Ron work on a paper airplane; Karen watches Mark and Ron. They aren't too disruptive, but the parents try to get them to pay attention. They settle down when the pastor begins.)

Pastor: Tonight's Bible study topic is "The Family of God."

(Some of the kids groan.)

Pastor: Before we actually get into that portion of the study, though, I'd like to spend some time talking about what it really means to be a family. So please break into your groups, and start the discussion there. Remember, young-married couples are in the library, seniors in the choir room, parents of preschoolers in the nursery, parents of teens in the office reception area, and teens, of course, in the youth room.

(Characters get up and move their chairs. Parents form a semicircle on one side of the stage, facing the audience. Teens form a more informal arrangement on the opposite side of the stage, sitting both on chairs and on the floor, and face the audience. As one group talks, the other group freezes.)

Karen: *(Cheerfully)* OK, so what does it mean to be a family?

Ron: *(Laughing)* Rules!

Jen: Having to be perfect.

Karen: Come on, you guys, this is supposed to be serious.

Ron: *(Takes a more serious tone.)* I am serious. I never get a break from my dad. He's always complaining about something.

Bob: I know the feeling.

Ron: I think he just likes hassling me. I know the Bible says we're supposed to honor our parents, but he gets mad about the stupidest things. I mean, the other night I was late getting back from hockey practice because a couple of guys from the college team were there and showed us some moves. *(Jumps up and fakes blocking a shot.)* It was great! But when I got home, my dad was sitting in the living room with the lights out. *(Sits down, imitating Mike.)*

Jen: I hate it when they do that kind of stuff.

Ron: I was all psyched to tell him, but he wouldn't even talk about it. He just said, *(imitating Mike again, using a low, slow voice)* "Where have you been? You missed dinner. Just go upstairs." *(As himself)* Fine!

Mark: Did you ask him why he was so mad?

Ron: No way. If he wants to blow me off, go for it. That's the last time I try to tell him anything.

(Kids freeze. Scene switches to parents.)

Ilsbeth: Well, this is quite a topic. Who'd like to start?

Chris: Does he want us to talk about traditional families, blended families, or single-parent families or what?

Carlie: Probably all of them.

Ilsbeth: What does the Bible say about families? *(Opens her Bible and flips pages.)*

Robert: I think there's that "spare the rod and spoil the child" thing.

Mike: Is there any advice in there about impossible kids?

Carlie: Having problems with Ron again?

Mike: Ever since my wife died, it seems as though we're always at odds. I can't get him to listen. When I try to talk to him, he just ignores me or gets mad.

Robert: *(Kindly)* How long has it been?

Mike: *(Gets up and paces a little.)* Meaghan died five years ago last week. It's so hard to understand. One day she was there; the next day she wasn't. *(Pauses.)* That's one of the things I'm upset with Ron about. We always go out for dinner on the anniversary of Meaghan's death. Just me and him. It's a tradition. Last week he was so late getting back from practice that it was too late to do anything.

Carlie: Was he apologetic?

Mike: *(Sits.)* No. There I was, waiting all evening, getting more and more scared that something had happened to him. I even called the ice rink, but nobody was in the office. I sat there in the living room in the dark and cried. I was so afraid something happened to him. Then, when he finally got home, he wanted to talk about hockey.

Robert: That's rough.

Ilsbeth: Did you confront him about it?

Mike: No, I couldn't. I guess I didn't want him to see me crying. It just hurt so much that he didn't remember.

Carlie: Ron really misses his mom. I'm surprised he'd forget. When was the last time you talked to him about the dinner?

Mike: Oh, I don't know. I'm not sure we really did. We just always go. It didn't occur to me to have to remind him.

(Parents freeze, and the scene switches to kids.)

Karen: At least your dad cares. My mom wouldn't notice if I never showed up again. She's always too busy with her job. *(Gets up and turns away from the group.)*

Jen: Sure she would.

Karen: You know it's true, Jen. *(Turns back.)* Remember last summer?

Jen: Oh, yeah.

Mark: What happened?

Karen: We were going to this concert in Riverton.

Bob: Oh, really?

Jen: *(Grabs the front of his shirt.)* Bob, don't you dare tell Mom and Dad about this.

Bob: *(Smiling slyly)* Why not?

Jen: *(Lets go of him and says smugly.)* Because if you do, I'll tell them about Sherry West.

Bob: *(Backing off)* OK, OK! It's our little secret.

Karen: *(Sits.)* So anyway, Jen tells her parents that she's spending the night with me, and we sneak out to the concert. Well, of course the stupid car won't start after the concert. It's like two in the morning, and here we are with no money, totally lost, and we spent the night in the car.

Jen: It was so scary!

Karen: We weren't scared.

(Jen gives her a look.)

Karen: OK, we were scared. The important thing is that by the time we had a friend drive up there, loan us some money, and got the car fixed, it was after lunch the next day. My mom didn't even look up from the computer when I came in. She just asked how church was. She didn't even know I hadn't been home!

Bob: That's so great!

Karen: *(Slouches down.)* It's not great. It stinks. I'm going to be so glad to go away to college. Then I won't ever have to think about her again. I won't have to pretend that she cares.

(Kids freeze. Scene switches to parents.)

Ilsbeth: At least you know what's going on in your kid's life. My job takes up so much of my time that I hardly ever get to see Karen, let alone be involved in her life.

Carlie: Well, she's with Jen a lot.

Ilsbeth: *(Reaches over and pats Carlie's arm.)* I'm glad about that. At least I know they're not out doing something foolish. But it makes me sad. I miss her.

Chris: Is there just no way to cut back on your hours?

Ilsbeth: I wish I could. In so many ways this job has been an answer to prayer, but with the time it takes…Frankly, it's the only way I'll have enough money to send her to college. I know she really wants to go. I just want to be a good parent and give her everything she needs.

Mike: I'm sure she understands.

(Parents freeze, and the scene switches to kids.)

Mark: *(To Bob)* So why do you think it'd be so great to be ignored?

Bob: Because it's impossible being *her* big brother! *(Gives Jen a little push.)*

Jen: *(Stands up.)* Oh, yeah? Try being your little sister! *(Imitating Robert and Carlie, vocally and physically.)* "Bob gets straight A's in math—you need to try harder. Bob always cleans his room when we ask him—why can't you be more like him?"

Bob: *(Sarcastically)* Poor baby! *(Standing and imitating Robert and Carlie)* "Jen is looking to you to set the example. Your sister is relying on your good judgment. You're responsible for your sister."

Jen: *(Right in Bob's face)* You get to do everything first!

Bob: *(In Jen's face)* You get to do everything because I had to convince Mom and Dad to let me do it in the first place!

Ron: *(Pulling them apart)* Back off!

Bob: *(Bitterly)* She's their baby. She never has to work for anything, they just give it to her.

Jen: They think he's perfect. I'm never going to be as good as him. It's no wonder that Cain guy in the Bible killed his brother!

(Kids freeze, and the scene switches to parents.)

Carlie: *(Slowly walks around behind Robert's chair and puts her hands on his shoulders.)* I wish our kids understood how blessed they are to have each other. All they ever seem to do is fight.

Chris: That's the way siblings are, isn't it? I remember fighting with my brothers.

Carlie: I suppose. But it just seems like there's some kind of rivalry between them. I'm afraid they really don't like each other.

Robert: *(Puts his hand on one of Carlie's.)* They're both such good kids. Bob works really hard. He's so responsible.

Carlie: Jen could certainly take a few lessons from him, but she's her own person.

Robert: Yeah, Jen's kind of a free spirit, so we let her do her own thing as much as possible.

Mike: It sounds like you understand them pretty well. I wonder why they feel so negative about each other.

(Parents freeze, and the scene switches to kids.)

Mark: Kind of makes me glad I don't have any brothers or sisters.

Bob: *(Walks through the group and gives Mark a little shove as he passes.)* That would sure mess up your perfect little life.

Mark: What's that supposed to mean?

Ron: You're the one with the Father of the Year.

Mark: *(Stands up.)* I am not!

Jen: You have to admit, you and your dad get along really good.

Mark: Well, I guess we do.

Karen: Why is it so easy for you and so hard for me?

Mark: *(Kneels next to Karen.)* It's not exactly easy. I mean, we fight and stuff, too. But we do stuff and talk. It's not like he's the coolest dad, but he's OK.

Ron: *(Sarcastically)* Isn't that sweet? Daddy's little boy.

Karen: Be quiet. You're just jealous because you don't talk to your dad at all.

Jen: *(To Mark)* What kind of stuff do you do?

Mark: You know, we go to games or watch movies or whatever. *(Pauses.)* You're going to think this is stupid, but we read the Bible together every night.

Bob: What?

Mark: It's kind of this ritual, you know, before bed.

Karen: *(Wistfully)* That's so great.

(Kids freeze. Scene switches to parents.)

Ilsbeth: So, Chris, are things OK with Mark?

Chris: Mostly. We have our ups and downs.

Mike: You two really seem to get along, though.

Chris: Yeah, we do pretty well.

Carlie: *(Moving back to her chair)* What's your secret?

Chris: I'm not sure. We try to spend time together, talk, and deliberately plan things. And we always read the Bible together at night.

Robert: How in the world did you manage that?

Chris: It actually started when Mark was having trouble with his reading. We decided to work on it a little every night, and the Bible seemed like a logical choice.

Ilsbeth: How's his reading?

Chris: Oh, he's doing fine now. That was a few years ago.

Mike: And you're still reading together?

Chris: We just never stopped. It's nice. Even if we don't know what else to talk about, we can usually talk about something we've been reading.

(Parents freeze. Scene switches back to kids.)

Ron: I don't care what we read. I don't think my dad and I could talk about anything.

Karen: My mom doesn't care enough to do something like that.

Jen: Maybe some parents just never get it.

Bob: Ours sure don't.

Karen: They'll never see things from our side.

(Kids freeze. Scene switches to parents.)

Mike: I guess I'm just doomed to have a bad relationship with Ron. Maybe things would've been different if Meaghan hadn't died.

Ilsbeth: Maybe it'll happen later. I keep thinking once I get Karen though college…

Carlie: Isn't it usually like this? Parents not understanding their kids?

Robert: I suppose, but I'd like to think there was some kind of solution.

(Parents freeze.)

◆◆◆ Discussion Activity ◆◆◆

Have kids discuss the following questions:

● **What made Mark's relationship with his dad different from the others?**

● **What advice would you give to the other kids to help them improve their relationships with their parents?**

● **Why do you think the parents were having a tough time seeing from the perspective of their kids?**

Have kids each think of a time when they got into a fight with one of their parents or a sibling. Encourage each person to look at the fight from the other person's perspective and to think about what the other person might have been feeling.

Have the kids share what they might have done differently to prevent the argument.

Ask: **How does seeing it from another perspective help you come up with alternatives?**

Have the kids come up with three things they can do or say to help calm the situation the next time they start to argue with someone in their families.

Say: **You've probably heard "Honor your father and mother" before. There's more to the verse than that. There is a reason for obeying your parents.**

Have them look up Ephesians 6:1-4, and then ask:

● **According to these verses, how should family members treat one another?**

● **What are some things you can do to make it easier to do this?**

In The Name of Friendship

Scripture: Proverbs 17:17 and John 15:12-15

Topic: Friendship

Setting: Outdoors, somewhere in a city

Props: You'll need a small bag containing three cans of spray paint, as well as the sound of a police-car siren (easily accomplished with a tape recording).

Characters:
Scott—the "tough" teen
Dennis—Scott's buddy
Josh—an uncertain teen
Gene—Josh's friend
Aaron—Josh's friend
David—Josh's friend
First Officer
Second Officer
A few other teens

◆◆◆ Script ◆◆◆

(As the scene opens, Josh, Gene, Aaron, David and a few other teens are hanging out together, talking. Scott and Dennis enter stage right, and stand apart from the crowd, obviously making fun of them.)

Gene: *(Pointing)* There's Scott and Dennis. I wonder why they're here?

Josh: *(Nervously)* Well, uh, I invited them.

Gene: You did? Why?

Josh: Well, Scott and I got to talking. He's really pretty cool. I think we have the wrong idea about him.

Gene: Maybe! But I wouldn't be so quick to judge on just one conversation.

David: He may seem OK, but some of his actions are so mean.

Aaron: *(Nodding)* Yesterday he knocked all of my books out of my hands, for no reason.

Josh: *(Quickly)* I asked him about that. He said it was an accident.

Gene: *(Incredulous)* Accident? I think not! I saw it myself. It was deliberate.

Josh: *(Squirming)* Well, maybe.

Scott: *(Yelling from the other side of the stage)* Hey, Josh! Come on over here with us. Quit hanging around those losers.

David: Losers? *(Shakes his head.)* He's changed, huh?

Dennis: Yeah, come on, Josh. We're going to have some fun.

Aaron: Your new buddy wants you, Josh. And from what I hear, he has no patience, so you'd better get over there. Come on, David, let's go.

(All exit stage right, except for Gene, Josh, Dennis, and Scott.)

Scott: Are you coming or not, Josh?

Gene: Go ahead, Josh, but be careful. Please.

Josh: He's just in a hurry, Gene. Maybe tomorrow we can do something, OK? Or maybe you can come with us.

Gene: *(Shakes head.)* Sorry, friend. I don't hang around people like Scott and Dennis. They're just bad news. I want real friends *(punches Josh in the arm)*—like you.

Dennis: You deaf or what, Josh? Come on!

(Josh makes his way over to Dennis and Scott. Dennis has a small bag with three cans of spray paint. Gene makes his way stage right, almost out of sight. He watches Josh, Scott, and Dennis closely, but not obviously.)

Josh: Hi, guys. Say, Dennis, what's in the sack?

Scott: *(With a huge grin)* This evening's entertainment.

Josh: Entertainment? What do you mean?

Scott: *(Points stage left.)* See that white wall over there?

Josh: You mean the one they just repainted last week?

(Scott punches Dennis in the arm. Dennis winces.)

Scott: Yeah, that's the one. I told you he was a smart one, Dennis, didn't I? *(Dennis nods.)*

Josh: So, what's with the wall?

Scott: *(Grinning)* We're going to decorate it for them. Plain white is so ugly.

Josh: *(Bewildered)* Decorate? How?

Scott: Show him, Dennis.

(Dennis pulls out the spray paint. Gene gasps from the other side of the stage.)

Scott: *(Looking around)* What was that? *(Spies Gene.)* You! What are you doing over there? *(Jogs to center stage.)*

Gene: Just hanging out. What are you doing?

Scott: You know exactly what we're doing, and if you breathe a word of it to anyone, I'll hurt you. *(Pauses.)* Understand?

Gene: *(Shrugs, but appears visibly shaken.)* Yeah, I understand.

Scott: *(Jogs back to the other two.)* Let's go!

Josh: I'm not so sure I want to do this.

Scott: *(Grabs spray can from Dennis and shoves it into Josh's hand.)* Too late now, bud. You're in. *(Pushes Josh hard.)* Move it!

(Josh, Scott, and Dennis exit stage left. Josh glances back at Gene as if asking for help. Gene crosses almost all the way to stage left.)

Gene: Poor Josh! We tried to warn him. Oh, man! Look at that! Josh is just standing there, not doing anything. That's good for him, I guess. At least, I hope it is.

(Siren sounds.)

Gene: Oh, no! The police!

(Josh, Scott, and Dennis run across the stage, followed by two police officers. Gene slides over stage right, to his previous spot.)

First Officer: Halt!

(Josh, Scott, and Dennis stop. Josh looks frightened. Scott and Dennis act as if nothing is wrong. The Second Officer stands by the boys, and the First Officer stands center stage.)

First Officer: What were you boys doing over there?

Josh: *(Quickly)* I wasn't doing anything, honest!

Scott: *(Stage whisper)* Shut up, if you know what's good for you.

First Officer: *(Surveys the three boys.)* Guess I need to talk to you guys separately. You *(points to Dennis)*, come here. *(Dennis crosses over to him.)* So, what do you have to say?

Dennis: Nothing. Why should I say anything?

First Officer: Go back over there by the other officer. *(Points to Josh, but speaks more kindly.)* You, son, come here.

Josh: Me?

First Officer: Yes, you.

Scott: *(Stage whisper, threateningly)* Remember what I said, Josh.

(Josh crosses to First Officer.)

First Officer: Tell me, son, what were you doing? Did you spray paint that wall?

Josh: *(Surprised)* No, sir! I did not!

First Officer: Then, who did?

(Josh just shakes his head.)

First Officer: *(Pointing at Scott)* All right, come on over, you.

(Scott saunters across the stage.)

First Officer: I don't suppose you saw who did it?

Scott: *(Stage whisper)* Yeah, I did. It was those other two, but I didn't have anything to do with it.

First Officer: *(Looks disbelieving.)* Really. Hmmmm. Well, let's take them in.

Gene: Officer! Wait! *(Crosses stage to First Officer.)*

First Officer: There's another one? Where'd you come from, son?

Gene: I saw the whole thing, officer, and Josh here *(pointing to Josh)* was pushed into going by these other two. He never even opened his can.

Scott: That's gonna cost you, Gene.

(Second Officer leads Scott and Dennis away stage left. Josh crosses over to Gene and First Officer.)

First Officer: Quiet! Take them to the car; leave Josh here. *(Turns to Gene.)* Thanks, son. That's what we thought. Scott and Dennis here are old hands at this, and they've told us this story before. *(Pats Josh on the shoulder.)* That's some friend you've got there, son. I'd say you'd better keep him. *(Exits.)*

Josh: Gene! Why'd you tell? You know Scott will be after you.

Gene: *(Smiles.)* Maybe, but I just couldn't stand by and let you take the blame for what he did. It wasn't right. You're my friend.

Josh: Thanks, Gene. I hope I can be a friend like you.

◆◆◆ Discussion Activity ◆◆◆

Have kids form groups of five to seven and ask each group to sit in a circle. Pass out a piece of paper and a pencil or pen to each person. Ask kids to write their names at the top of their papers and then each pass the paper to the person on the right. The person who receives the paper will write one good friendship quality about the person whose name is on the top. Continue passing the paper to the next person on the right until each group member has written a positive friendship quality on each paper.

After the papers have returned to their owners, say: **Look at the qualities people listed about you.** Ask: **Do any qualities surprise you?**

Read John 15:12-15. Say: **Jesus called his disciples friends right after he predicted that they would desert him. Jesus believed his disciples should love one another. The kind of love the disciples had for one another is what we often call friendship. Two of the most important things you can do as a teenager are to have the right kind of friends and to be the right kind of friends.** Ask:

● **Proverbs 17:17 says, "A friend loves at all times." What do you think that means?**

● **What qualities does a real friend have?**

Louder Than Words

Scripture: Mark 9:35

Topic: Service

Setting: A school cafeteria and a classroom

Props: You'll need a table with chairs for the lunchroom, chairs to resemble a classroom, and some schoolbooks. Set up the lunchroom on one side of the stage and the classroom on the other side.

Characters:
  Matt—a teenage boy that came to school today without his lunch money or notebook paper
  Lena—a teenage girl with a bad attitude
  Sally—a deaf teenage girl with a servant's heart
  Jenny—a teenage girl in the cafeteria
  Jeff—a teenage boy in the cafeteria
  Ruben—a teenage boy in the classroom
  Tyrone—a teenage boy in the classroom
  Teacher—a female or male, Mr. or Ms. Barnett

◆◆◆ Script ◆◆◆

(The scene opens in the cafeteria with the teacher signing or pretending to sign to Sally. This scene can be improvised since it is just to let the audience know that Sally is deaf. Sally and the Teacher remain in the background while the scene focuses on Matt and the students he talks to.)

Matt: Hey, Jenny, can I borrow fifty cents from you?

Jenny: Sorry, I want to buy a Coke after school.

Matt: Jeff, do you have fifty cents I can borrow?

Jeff: Do I look like a bank to you?

(Jeff walks off, and Matt sits down at a table.)

Lena: *(Sits down next to Matt with a lunch tray.)* Matt, why aren't you eating lunch?

Matt: I don't have any money today.

Lena: Oh, well! That starving look is sort of becoming on you!

Matt: Ha ha! You wouldn't have an extra fifty cents would you?

Lena: Are you kidding? I don't give handouts!

Matt: I'm not looking for a handout, just a loan until tomorrow.

Lena: No! I only have fifty cents, and I'm going to buy an ice cream with it when I finish eating.

(Sally, the deaf girl, comes and sits down at the table beside them and opens her lunch.)

Matt: Well then, could I have one of your french fries?

Lena: No, Matt! You are such a loser!

(She gets up and walks away. Matt and Sally look at each other and smile; then Matt watches Lena walk away, shakes his head, and puts his head in his hands. Sally pretends to divide a sandwich, taps Matt on the shoulder, and offers him half of it. She smiles and Matt takes the sandwich.)

Matt: Thank you.

(He smiles. Once he finishes the sandwich, he picks up his books and waves goodbye to Sally. As he turns to leave, Lena comes from the opposite direction, accidentally bumps into him, and knocks the books out of his hand.)

Lena: Why don't you watch out where you're going?

Matt: Me? You're the one who ran into me!

Lena: Oh, please!

Matt: *(Bends down to pick up his books.)* Well, aren't you at least going to help me pick them up?

Lena: Pick them up yourself, jerk!

(Matt looks at her in disbelief. Sally walks over and helps Matt pick up his books.)

Matt: Thanks.

(Sally smiles and then walks off. People just look at her and whisper. A bell rings, and all the students go sit down on the opposite side of the stage, pretending to be in a classroom.)

Teacher: Students, take out a sheet of paper for a pop quiz.

Matt: Pop quiz? On a Monday? *(Fumbling through his notebook)* Oh great! I'm out of paper. Say, Tyrone, do you have a piece of paper I can borrow?

Tyrone: Sorry, man, I barely have enough for myself.

Matt: Hey, Ruben, do you have a piece of paper I can borrow?

Ruben: Man, I was hoping I could borrow some from you!

Matt: Sorry! *(Looks at Lena, who is sitting on the opposite side of him.)* Lena. Lena! Can I borrow a sheet of paper for the quiz?

Lena: What is with you today? You don't have money, and you don't have any paper. It's not exactly a good way to start out your week. Do you just expect everybody to give you everything?

Matt: I'm just asking for one sheet of paper.

Lena: *(Mockingly)* I'm just asking for one sheet of paper.

Matt: You don't have to get nasty about it.

Lena: Look, Matt, my parents work hard to be able to buy *my* school supplies and give *me* lunch money. I don't think they would appreciate it if I went around giving it all away!

Matt: I don't ask every day. It's just that I forgot my lunch money today, and I just happened to have run out of notebook paper, that's all!

Lena: Whatever! You're such a loser!

Matt: Never mind! I would rather get a zero on the stinking test than borrow anything from you anyway!

Teacher: *(Passing out the quiz)* Please don't write on the quiz; pass it in with your paper when you have finished. *(She pretends to sign to Sally.)* OK, is everyone ready?

Matt: I'm not, Ms. Barnett. I don't have a sheet of paper.

Teacher: Matt, you know you need to come to class with paper and a pen.

Matt: I know. I thought I had some in my notebook.

Lena: Why don't you ask your little girlfriend over there? *(She points toward Sally and everybody laughs.)*

Matt: She's not my girlfriend!

(Sally looks at him for a minute and then understands that he is out of paper and offers him several sheets of her paper. Embarrassed that she has helped him so much already, he slowly takes the paper and everyone laughs.)

Matt: Thank you.

Teacher: When you have finished the test, you may be excused. *(She pretends to sign to Sally. One by one the students finish and exit. Lena and Ruben remain behind talking quietly to one another. Sally and Matt finish last. After they hand in their papers, the Teacher exits.)*

Matt: Well, here we are again. Thanks a lot for the paper! It seems like I am always thanking you.

(Sally just looks at him.)

Matt: I wish I knew how to communicate with you. *(He reaches out and shakes her hand.)* Thanks!

(Sally smiles, waves goodbye, and walks off. Lena walks up to Matt.)

Lena: I'm so glad I'm not like her! She's plain, she's not popular, and she can't even communicate with people!

Matt: That's where you're wrong, Lena. Sally communicates with me quite well! She communicates a kindness and a joy that I can't understand. She knows what it means to care for people! She is an incredible person, always willing to be a servant! You know, I guess it's true what they say about actions speaking louder than words!

(As he walks off in one direction, Lena gives him a sharp look and walks off in the other direction.)

◆◆◆ Discussion Activity ◆◆◆

Before the discussion activity, you'll need to make enough pre-cut hearts from red construction paper for each participant to have one.

Read Mark 9:35 out loud and ask:

- What did Jesus mean when he said, "If anyone wants to be first, he must be the very last, and the servant of all"?

Say: We can often think of reasons why we can't help others. Sometimes we are just too caught up in our own activities to see their needs. The Bible reminds us, however, that we are to watch out for the needs of others.

Ask:

- Why does the Bible emphasize that we should help those in need?
- At what times do you find yourself too busy to help others?

Read the poem *The World Is Mine* to the group, and then hand out pre-cut hearts made of red construction paper. Give kids a pen or pencil, and instruct them to write down all the things they can think of that keep them from serving God as they should. Also, have them write on their paper hearts a response to each of the following questions:

- Who do you need to be nicer to?
- Who needs your help?
- What can you do in your life right now that will help you develop a servant's heart?

Instruct kids to keep their construction paper hearts as a reminder to watch out for and help those in need.

The World Is Mine

Today, upon a bus, I saw a lovely girl with golden hair.
I envied her, she seemed so gay; I wished I were as fair.
When suddenly she rose to leave, I saw her hobble down the aisle;
She had one leg, and wore a crutch, and as she passed—a smile.
O God, forgive me when I whine; I have two legs. The world is mine.

And when I stopped to buy some sweets, the lad who sold them had such charm.
I talked with him—he seemed so glad—if we are late 'twould do no harm.
And as I left he said to me, "I thank you. You have been so kind.
It's nice to talk with folks like you. You see," he said, "I'm blind."
O God, forgive me when I whine. I have two eyes. The world is mine.

Later, walking down the street, I saw a child with eyes of blue.
He stood and watched the others play; seemed he knew not what to do.
I stopped a moment, then I said: "Why don't you join the others, Dear?"
He looked ahead without a word, and then I knew—He could not hear.
O God, forgive me when I whine. I have two ears. The world is mine.

With legs to take me where I'd go,
With eyes to see the sunset's glow,
With ears to hear what I would know.
O God, forgive me when I whine. I'm blessed indeed. The world is mine.

(Author unknown, from *Ageless Inspirations,* compiled by Ellie Busha)

The Okra Windbag Show

Scripture: John 13:34

Topic: Family

Setting: A television talk show

Props: You'll need chairs for each character to sit in, bubble gum for Molly, and a bowl of okra (or something that looks like okra).

Characters:

Okra Windbag—the host of the show

Jennifer—a girl-next-door type of teenager who has trouble getting along with her parents

Lisa—Jennifer's mother

Abbie—Okra's television producer who stands to the side watching the show

Molly—a teenager who wears black, has several tattoos and body piercings, and who has been caught smoking at school

Ms. Strictly—Molly's teacher at school

 **◆◆◆ Script ◆◆◆**

Abbie: *(Counts.)* Three, two, one…

Okra: Welcome to the *Okra Windbag Show*. It's everyone's favorite daytime talk show. Today, young people from across the country have come to talk about their families. Our first guest is Jennifer. She wrote in and told us that she can't get along with her parents. Ladies and gentlemen please welcome Jennifer.

(Okra prompts the audience to applaud as Jennifer enters and sits down next to Okra.)

Okra: Welcome to our show, Jennifer.

Jennifer: Thanks.

Okra: Well, Jennifer, you wrote and told me that you're having a problem getting along with your mom and her husband.

Jennifer: I don't really have a problem, Okra; they do. They just need to get off my case!

Okra: What do you mean "off your case"?

Jennifer: They are always griping at me and bossing me around!

Okra: In what way?

Jennifer: Well, they are always telling me what to do. But when I do it, it's never good enough!

Okra: Oh? How's that?

Jennifer: They always find something wrong with everything I do. Either I didn't do it right, I didn't do it long enough, or hard enough, or something. Stuff like that!

Okra: What kind of things do they tell you to do? Clean your room? Come home at a certain time? Jump off a cliff? Eat poison? What?

Jennifer: *(Jokingly)* Yeah, all that stuff!

(Okra laughs.)

Okra: Can you be a little more specific than just "stuff"?

Jennifer: OK! For example, if my mom tells me to clean my room, I will do my best to get it done. But when I get finished, does she say "good job" or "thank you"? Noooo…she says, "Why haven't you washed the dishes?" Or Roy will gripe at me because I haven't folded the clothes in the dryer. Stuff like that! They just get on my nerves because they're always griping at me!

Okra: I see. Now, let me clarify for the audience that Roy is your mom's husband but not your father. Right? He is your stepfather?

Jennifer: He is definitely not my father!

Okra: OK. Why don't we bring your mom out here and hear what she has to say?

Jennifer: Whatever!

Okra: Please give a warm welcome to Jennifer's mother, Lisa.

(Okra has the audience applaud as Lisa enters.)

Okra: Now, Lisa , I understand that you and Jennifer aren't getting along right now.

Lisa: No, we're not.

Okra: Jennifer feels that nothing she does is good enough and that you and your husband are always upset with her. What are your thoughts on that?

Lisa: Well, Okra, Lisa is exaggerating. We only complain when she doesn't finish her chores or ignores what we tell her.

Jennifer: Oh, right! You gripe at me all the time, no matter what I do!

Lisa: Well, if you would do what you're supposed to, we wouldn't have to gripe, would we?

Jennifer: I do what you tell me, and you still gripe at me. And you always take Roy's side on everything! You never listen to me!

Lisa: That's not true!

Jennifer: Yes it is! He hates me and you always take his side!

(Jennifer and Lisa ad lib an argument…he hates me…no he doesn't…yes he does…you hate him…and so forth.)

Okra: *(Tries to interrupt them.)* Lisa…Jennifer…Lisa! Jennifer! Hold on…wait a minute.

(The two stop arguing and listen to Okra.)

Okra: Now, we just went from "you gripe at me all the time" to "he hates me." I think there are some underlying problems here that we need to address. Lisa, how long have you and Roy been married?

Lisa: Five months.

Okra: Has there been tension from the beginning?

Lisa: Yes, I guess there has, Okra. Jennifer has never liked Roy.

Jennifer: Why should I? He is a jerk!

Lisa: He is not a jerk! Why do you have to be so rude to him?

(They improvise another argument over whether Lisa's husband is a jerk or not.)

Okra: Wait, wait, wait, wait! Lisa, did you two discuss this before you married Roy?

Lisa: I tried, Okra, but Jennifer is too stubborn to listen to me. She doesn't understand that Roy is good for us, both of us. He helps us put food on the table, pays the bills, buys her school clothes, and he wants the best for both of us. I couldn't do all that by myself, and her father has never helped us. *(Jennifer rolls her eyes.)*

Jennifer: Roy wants what's best for him, and he never buys me anything!

Lisa: And I guess you think those clothes you're wearing came from the Goodwill?

(They argue again about Roy. Okra whistles and they stop.)

Okra: Jennifer, do you have a relationship with your father?

Jennifer: I'd like to, but he never comes around, because my mother won't let him! She won't let me have anything to do with him!

Lisa: That's not true, Jennifer. Your dad doesn't come around because he chooses not to.

Jennifer: Probably because you treated him like you treat me!

(She begins to cry and runs off the stage. Lisa begins to cry too.)

Okra: It seems that the problems may be a little more serious than we realized. *(She walks over and puts a hand on Lisa's shoulder.)* Lisa, how about if our producer sets up an appointment with someone to help your family through this. Would that be OK?

Lisa: I would like that.

Okra: Fine. Abbie, can you please help Lisa? Let's take her backstage to talk with Jennifer and see if we can find someone to help them work through these problems.

(Abbie motions for Lisa to follow her, and Okra watches while they exit. Once they have gone, she introduces her next guest.)

Okra: Our next guest is Molly, who has been caught smoking but says her parents don't care. Please help me welcome Molly. *(Leads audience in applause as Molly enters and sits down.)* Hello, Molly. It's good to have you on our show.

Molly: No problem.

Okra: OK, Molly, you were caught smoking. Who caught you?

Molly: My English teacher, Ms. Strictly.

Okra: Where were you when she caught you smoking?

Molly: I was in the girls restroom at school.

Okra: That sounds serious. How many times have you been caught?

(Molly shrugs.)

Okra: You know what? Ms. Strictly is here with us today. Why don't we bring her out and see what she has to say about all this.

(Molly shrugs.)

Okra: Ms. Strictly, come on out here!

(Okra has the audience applaud as Ms. Strictly enters and sits next to Molly.)

Okra: Thank you for joining our show today. Molly has told us that you have caught her smoking in the girls restroom. How many times has this happened?

(Molly appears not to care.)

Ms. Strictly: Unfortunately, Okra, it has happened many times.

(Molly chews gum, blows a bubble, and pops it as she gives Ms. Strictly a nasty look.)

Okra: What do you do when you catch her?

Ms. Strictly: Well, the first time, I just gave her a warning, thinking that maybe she wouldn't do it again. The second time it happened, I sent her to the principal and he called her parents. The third time, she was suspended for a few days. Since then, we have tried different things, but nothing seems to be working.

Okra: Molly, don't you care if you get in trouble?

Molly: Not really.

Okra: What did your parents say when you got caught smoking? Did they punish you?

Molly: They like, don't care, 'cause like they both smoke.

Okra: I see. Have your parents warned you about the dangers of smoking?

Molly: Do I like know that smoking causes cancer? Is that what you mean?

Okra: Well yes, among other lung diseases.

Ms. Strictly: Not to mention that smoking makes your teeth yellow, your breath stink, your clothes and hair smell like smoke, and is not healthy for the people around you. Have they discussed those things with you?

Molly: *(Gives Ms. Strictly a dirty look.)* I think that is like totally none of your business!

Okra: Now, Ms. Strictly, you wrote to us because you didn't feel like you were getting any help from Molly's family.

Ms. Strictly: That's right, Okra. They really don't seem to care about what Molly does.

Okra: Molly, we invited your parents to be here with us today, but they couldn't make it. Are they working?

Molly: No, they just like didn't want to be here. They totally don't care what I do!

Okra: Oh, I'm sure they care, Molly.

Molly: No they don't! As long as I stay out of their hair, they don't care what I do. I wish Ms. Strictly would just totally stay out of it. She's not my mother!

Ms. Strictly: I just want to help you, Molly.

Molly: I don't need any help, thank you!

Okra: Molly, I think Ms. Strictly is just concerned for you. Let me ask you a question. Why do you smoke?

(Molly shrugs and starts biting her nails.)

Okra: Would you like to quit?

(Molly shrugs again.)

Okra: You know, Molly, sometimes old habits are hard to break. I know, I almost never broke my habit of overeating. From the time I woke up to the time I went to bed at night, I craved okra. That's how I got my name! But now...now I have overcome that nasty habit! Why, you could set a bowl right here in front of me, and I wouldn't touch the stuff! Just to prove it to you, let's have Abbie bring out a bowl. Abbie, could you bring some okra out here please?

(Abbie brings a bowl of okra, hands it to Okra, and exits. Okra waves the bowl in front of her face and sniffs the okra.)

Okra: See, no problem. You have got to want to throw the habit away. *(She picks up a piece of okra and begins to stutter a little.)* Yep, no uh...no problem at all! *(She nervously holds it in her hand.)*

Molly: I don't really want to stop smoking; it relaxes me.

Okra: *(Okra becomes preoccupied with the okra and her mouth begins to water.)* Well, um...I...um...Ms. Strictly, would you care to comment?

Ms. Strictly: Molly, smoking is bad for you.

Molly: Well, it's like not your problem!

(While they talk, Okra sneaks a bite of the okra that she is holding and makes facial expressions that imply she is eating something delightful.)

Ms. Strictly: But, Molly, it is my problem. If you are going to continue to smoke at school, and if your own family won't intervene, someone needs to!

Molly: Leave my family out of this! It's totally my life!

Ms. Strictly: But we came here today to talk about your family's lack of concern!

(By now, Okra loses interest in the conversation and becomes consumed with eating the okra.)

Ms. Strictly: Right, Okra? *(Looks at Okra.)* Okra? What are you doing?

Okra: Huh? *(Realizes what she is doing.)* Oh my! I don't know what came over me! Please forgive me for gorging myself like that. I guess old habits are harder to break than I realized. *(Pauses to look at the okra as she licks her lips.)* Molly, I'm afraid Ms. Strictly is right; we want to discuss your family's lack of concern. It is customary for families to care about one another.

Ms. Strictly: You know, Molly, maybe your parents need your support to help them stop smoking. Their health is important to you, isn't it?

Molly: *(Shrugs.)* I don't know. I like totally don't really care one way or the other.

Okra: I'll tell you what. You go home and try caring about your family and encourage your folks to stop smoking. If it works, I'll have you back on the show in six months. If at that time all three of you have stopped smoking, our show will give you an all-expense-paid family vacation to anywhere in the United States to celebrate the occasion. The trip will also help your family build a more caring relationship with each other. Is it a deal?

Molly: *(Shrugs.)* I don't know…

Okra: I'll have our producer talk with your family about it. OK?

Molly: *(Shrugs.)* Like whatever!

Okra: All right. *(She speaks to Abbie, who is standing off to the side.)* Abbie, see what you can do to help Molly and her family get started on this, will you?

(Abbie waves in agreement.)

Okra: Ms. Strictly, thanks for writing to us about this situation.

Ms. Strictly: Thank you for listening, Okra.

Okra: Well, ladies and gentlemen, our last guest is George. But I'm afraid we have run out of time for today. I will tell you though that George lives in a perfect home with perfect people. His only problem is that he doesn't like the okra that his mom serves with every meal. *(She walks over and picks up a piece of okra while talking.)* Can you imagine that? Poor George! He really does have a serious problem! Maybe we will bring him back another time! I guess that about wraps things up for today. Join us tomorrow when our topic will be, "How to tell your spouse that he or she has morning breath." Until next time *(she takes a bite of the okra)*, I'm Okra Windbag reminding you to make someone smile. *(Audience applauds.)*

◆◆◆ Discussion Activity ◆◆◆

Begin the discussion by asking:
- **Which one of the characters do you most relate to and why:**
- **Jennifer, who feels she can never please her parents?**
- **Molly, whose family doesn't seem to care about one another?**
- **Or George, who has a perfect family with very few problems?**

Have some of the students share what life is like in their families, both positive and negative aspects.

Next, have someone silently flicker the lights in the room. Say: **Imagine that a natural disaster has just occurred and that no one outside this room survived. Your families are gone. What would you miss about them?** End by reading John 13:34.

The GSS Association

Scripture: Luke 10:25-37 and John 15:12

Topic: Love

Setting: A church support-group meeting

Props: You'll need a podium, folding chairs, portable table, snacks (if desired), foam cups, a plate, a cap with a bill, and tissues. The podium should be located stage left, and several folding chairs at stage right in two rows. Behind the folding chairs, set up the refreshment table.

Characters:
Bill—the leader
Sandra—a member
Charlie—a member
Ed—a member
Tom—a member
Dave—a member
Joan—a member
Lucy—a visitor
Some other members

◆◆◆ Script ◆◆◆

(Bill is standing at the podium when the meeting begins. Joan is sitting on one of the chairs nearest the audience. Lucy is sitting in the back row, watching everyone with surprise and disbelief.)

Bill: Welcome to this week's meeting of the GSS Association. I trust everyone has helped themselves to the refreshments in the back?

(He surveys the group expectantly. Some of them nod. Others hold up foam cups.)

Bill: Good! Let's get started. My name is Bill, and I have GSS.

Crowd: Hi, Bill!

Bill: I'm also the president of our little organization. Let us begin by saying you should never be ashamed of admitting that you have GSS.

(Group whistles and applauds wildly. Bill holds up hand to restore quiet.)

Bill: Would anyone like to share his or her story?

Sandra: *(Stands.)* My name is Sandra, and I have *(voice breaks)* GSS.

Crowd: Ahhh...

Charlie: It's OK, Sandra, we love ya!

Ed: Yeah, Sandra, we're all friends here.

Sandra: *(Sniffling, wipes away tears.)* Yesterday, I let someone go ahead of me in the checkout line at the grocery store! *(She sits and cries. Those next to her pat her back and hand her tissues.)*

Charlie: We know how you feel, Sandra.

Ed: We sure do!

Bill: *(Looks expectantly at the crowd.)* Anyone else?

Tom: *(Stands. Twirls cap in hand and looks at floor.)* My name is Tom, and *(pauses and gulps)* I have GSS.

Charlie: *(Encouragingly)* We love ya, Tom!

Ed: Tell us your story, Tom.

Tom: I well, I...*(voice breaks.)* I gave a homeless family our grocery money. We barely ate until my next paycheck. *(Pauses, then speaks triumphantly.)* There I said it!

(Beaming, he sits as the crowd around him pats him on the back.)

Bill: For those of you who don't know Tom, we've been encouraging him to tell his story for weeks now. Tonight's the first time he has shared. Congratulations, Tom!

(Applauds, and the group joins in.)

Charlie: Way to go, Tom!

Ed: I knew you could do it!

Bill: *(Looks at crowd.)* Who's next?

Joan: *(Raises hand.)* I guess I am. *(Stands.)* My name is Joan, and...and, I have GSS.

Charlie: We love ya, Joan!

Ed: Tell us your story, Joan.

Joan: Just the other day *(looking at crowd apologetically)* I took my elderly neighbor to the doctor because she had no other ride. As a result I missed a meeting with a very important client. My boss was furious!

Crowd: Ahhh...

Joan: *(Holds up her hand.)* But, that's not all! I got fired over it! Now what am I going to do?

(She sits, weeping with her head in her hands. The others comfort her.)

Charlie: That's all right, Joan, we've all been there.

Ed: We know how you feel, Joan.

Bill: No need to be ashamed, Joan. We're here for you. How about one of our newest members? Dave?

Dave: *(Stands, goes to the podium, turns to face the crowd, and gives a small wave.)* Hi, my name is Dave. And I have GSS.

Charlie: Attaboy, Dave!

(Crowd laughs.)

Dave: My story's a little hard to tell. *(Looks at floor.)*

Ed: You can do it, man.

Dave: *(Looks up and smiles briefly.)* I knew I was different from my friends, but I didn't really know why. It first started by giving someone a penny who didn't have one.

Sandra: *(Stands.)* That's always one of the first warning signs. *(Sits.)*

Dave: *(Smiles again.)* Then, I started opening doors for people, especially the elderly and those with their hands full.

Joan: *(Stands and shakes head sadly.)* It didn't end there, did it? *(Sits.)*

Dave: *(Sadly)* No, it didn't. My friends noticed the difference in me. Some stopped calling. Others tried to keep me from leaving tips in the restaurants.

Ed: *(Incredulous)* You left tips?

(Dave nods.)

Ed: Man!

Charlie: Attaboy, Dave.

(Crowd giggles.)

Dave: *(Sighs.)* Then, the worst thing happened.

Bill: Go on, Dave, you can tell us.

Dave: I couldn't help it! See, there was this kid in the drug store. *(Defensively)* I only went in to buy some aspirin. And there was a long line. I was behind this kid, and he was crying.

Tom: *(Stands and interrupts.)* Kids are the worst! *(Sits.)*

Dave: It was one of those cries that made you know something was really wrong.

Joan: *(Sympathetically)* Oh, poor thing. *(Everyone glares at her.)* Sorry.

Dave: His mother apologized. Said he wasn't feeling well and she was trying to find the right medicine for him. I felt his forehead. He was really hot, and I noticed she only clutched a few dollars…

Sandra: *(Blurts out, horrified.)* No! You didn't!

Dave: *(Nods.)* Yes. *(Sighs.)* I took them to the clinic next door. I paid for his doctor bill. I even paid for his medicine.

(Crowd groans.)

Dave: I even used my car payment to do it. How am I going to make my car payment? *(Crowd groans even louder as Dave returns to his seat.)*

Lucy: *(Stands.)* Excuse me—may I say something?

Bill: *(Nods.)* We're always glad to hear from our visitors.

Charlie: You can talk to us.

Ed: Tell us your story, Lucy.

Lucy: Seems to me, you're all missing the point.

(Crowd gasps as she goes to the podium.)

Lucy: GSS is not a horrible disease.

Bill: *(Grudgingly)* Now, Lucy, you can't mean that. No one else acts like we do.

Lucy: *(Nods emphatically.)* I do mean it! Being a Good Samaritan is not a sickness.

Joan: *(Stands.)* It's not? How can you say that? Tom's family needs groceries, I lost my job, and Dave here *(points to Dave)* might lose his car!

(Crowd mumbles their agreement.)

Lucy: *(Smiling)* But, you see, you can help one another like you helped those folks. For instance, there's an opening at my workplace, Joan, that I'd be happy to recommend you for.

Joan: *(Incredulous)* You would?

Lucy: *(Nods.)* Yes, and Dave, if you hadn't helped that little boy, what would have happened?

Dave: *(Slowly)* I'm not sure. He was very sick.

Lucy: What's more important, your car or that little boy's health?

Bill: *(Blurting)* The boy, of course!

(Everyone stares at him. Lucy smiles.)

Lucy: That's right! Don't you think we could take up a small collection to help Tom and Dave here? And we could contact the local food pantry, too.

(The crowd murmurs agreement and nods at one another. Someone gets up, crosses to the snack table, gets a plate, and begins passing it among the members.)

Joan: And my neighbor really had no one else to take her—no one. *(Shakes head for emphasis.)*

Tom: And you should have seen that family. I wish now I could have done more for them.

Lucy: We're supposed to do good deeds and be friends to others. We are supposed to treat others like we want to be treated. We shouldn't call that a disease, and we don't have to hide from it.

(Bill stares at her uncomprehendingly.)

Sandra: *(Stands.)* No more hiding?

Lucy: No more hiding.

Charlie: *(Bewildered)* Well, whaddya know.

Ed: *(Surprised)* Ain't that something?

Bill: *(Hesitantly)* Are you sure, Lucy?

Lucy: I'm very sure. What do you think would happen if every Christian had the **G**ood **S**amaritan **S**yndrome?

◆◆◆ Discussion Activity ◆◆◆

Using whatever items are available, such as chairs, large toddler toys, and so forth, build a mini-obstacle course. Choose eight people from the group. Place the blindfold on at least one person, and have him or her try to go through the obstacle course without any assistance. Next, divide your group of eight into pairs. Blindfold one person in each pair, and have the other person lead the blindfolded partner through the obstacle course.

Ask:

● **What was it like for the first person to go through the obstacle course without help?**

● **If everyone took the time to help another person, what do you think the result would be?**

Read John 15:12. Ask: **What did Jesus mean when he said, "Love each other as I have loved you"?**

Read Luke 10:25-37. Ask:

● **Why did the Pharisee ask who his neighbor was?**

● **What is Jesus' definition of a neighbor?**

Obstacles in the Path

❧

The Tale of Mr. Hipp

Scripture: Matthew 7:3-5

Topic: Hypocrisy

Setting: This skit takes place in an imaginary kingdom. The narrator stands on a platform or box at the rear of the stage. Voices stand stage right, and Mr. Hipp moves from stage left.

Props: The King wears a bathrobe and a crown made of foil. Mr. Hipp uses a chair and reads a newspaper. Mr. Hipp also carries a small pouch with lettering that reads "Chewing Tobacco," which he pretends to use.

Characters:
Narrator—a female
Voices 1, 2, 3, 4, and 5—the chorus
Mr. Hipp—a young man
King Bob

◆◆◆ Script ◆◆◆

Narrator: Good evening, and welcome to our story. I am your narrator and these are the Voices. Together we will tell you a tale of hypocrisy.

Voice 1: *(In a stage whisper)* Did she say "hip-hop crazy"?

Voice 2: No! *Hypocrisy.* It means pretending to be something you're not.

Voice 3: It's like telling people to eat a healthy diet while you live on junk food.

Voice 1: Oh. Hypocrisy.

Narrator: As I was saying, this is a story about hypocrisy. Once upon a time in a tiny kingdom, there lived a man named Mr. Hipp.

Mr. Hipp: *(Enters stage left.)* Hello, everyone.

Voices 1, 2, 3, 4, and 5: Hello, Mr. Hipp.

Narrator: Mr. Hipp often pretended to be someone that he wasn't.

Mr. Hipp: I think people ought to respect each other's feelings. *(Sticks out his tongue at Voices.)* Get a life, you bunch of geeks.

Voices 1, 2, 3, 4, and 5: Cut that out!

Voice 3: How rude!

Voice 1: Hey, he's a hippo-crat.

Voice 3: *(To Voice 1)* That's *hypocrite.*

Voice 1: *(To Voice 3)* That's what I said.

Voices 2, 3, 4, and 5: Shhhh...!

Voice 1: Sorry.

Voice 4: Doesn't he know that hypocrisy is wrong?

Voice 5: Jesus said to correct your own faults before you go criticizing others.

Voice 3: Right! And get your own house in order before you start pointing out someone else's mess!

Voices 1, 2, 3, 4, and 5: This guy's got some learning to do!

Narrator: Mr. Hipp was especially hypocritical whenever the king appeared.

(King Bob enters.)

Voices 1, 2, 3, 4, and 5: His royal majesty, King Bob.

Voice 1: *Bob?* We're kidding, right?

Voices 2, 3, 4, and 5: Shhhh...!

Voice 4: It's an old family name.

Mr. Hipp: *(Bows to King Bob.)* Hello, your majesty. May I say what a beautiful robe you are wearing today. Is that *pure* polyester?

King Bob: Thank you. What a polite young man.

Narrator: But as soon as the King's back was turned...

(As King Bob turns to face the back of the stage, Mr. Hipp makes a gagging gesture by sticking his finger in his throat.)

Voices 1, 2, 3, 4, and 5: How obnoxious!

King Bob: *(Turns quickly to the others, just as Mr. Hipp pulls his finger out of his mouth.)* What?

Voices 1, 2, 3, 4, and 5: *(Disgusted)* Never mind.

Mr. Hipp: *(To King Bob)* They are so childish sometimes! *Wow,* aluminum foil! What a great crown.

Voices 1, 2, 3, 4, and 5: Oh, brother.

King Bob: *(To Mr. Hipp)* Young man, how would you like to work for me?

Mr. Hipp: Me, work for the King?

Voices 1, 2, 3, 4, and 5: *(Surprised)* Him, work for the King?

Mr. Hipp: *(Ignores the Voices.)* I'd be honored, your majesty.

King Bob: Fine. From now on you will be in charge of all the Voices in my kingdom.

Voices 1, 2, 3, 4, and 5: You mean us?

King Bob: Yes, you.

Voices 1, 2, 3, 4, and 5: *(Disappointed)* Oh, great!

Mr. Hipp: *(Very happy)* Oh, great!

King Bob: But if I find that you have been hypocritical, I will be very angry.

Mr. Hipp: Not to worry.

King Bob: Good! I must be going. Farewell, my loyal subjects.

Voices 1, 2, 3, 4, and 5: *(Depressed)* Goodbye, King Bob.

Mr. Hipp: *(Rubs his hands together gleefully.)* Don't worry about a thing.

Narrator: The situation soon became very grim for the Voices as Mr. Hipp settled into his new position. Before long, Mr. Hipp's hypocrisy was in full swing.

Mr. Hipp: *(Slouches in a chair reading a newspaper.)* Hey, look alive over there. Don't be so lazy.

Voices 1, 2, 3, 4, and 5: *(Very sad)* Yes, sir.

Mr. Hipp: *(Wads up the newspaper and throws it on the ground, then points stage right.)* Hey, Number 4, there's a gum wrapper on the ground near your foot. Put it in the trash. And stand up straight, you're slouching. *(Yawns.)* And wake up over there.

Voices 1, 2, 3, 4, and 5: *(Even sadder)* Yes, sir.

Mr. Hipp: *(Takes a pouch of chewing tobacco from his pocket and puts some in his mouth.)* I think we'll begin a campaign against smokeless tobacco. That should keep you five busy and make me look good.

Voice 5: But you chew tobacco all the time!

Voices 1, 2, 3, and 4: Yeah!

Mr. Hipp: So what? No one will ever know.

Narrator: The situation seemed hopeless. The Voices felt they would be stuck with Mr. Hipp forever. Then one day, while Mr. Hipp was being especially hypocritical…

Mr. Hipp: *(Now has untucked shirttails.)* Hey, Number 1, tuck in your shirt, and look alive. We've got a rally against prejudice in an hour. But first I've just *got* to tell you this great racial joke I heard today. *(King Bob enters stage left from behind Mr. Hipp.)*

Voices 1, 2, 3, 4, and 5: Your majesty!

Mr. Hipp: *(Doesn't believe them.)* Who, King *Bob?* Yeah, right. You can't fool me. What would he be doing here? That jerk is so clueless he actually thinks I respect him.

King Bob: *(Clears his throat.)* Mmm…

Mr. Hipp: *(His eyes widen as he slowly turns to face King Bob.)* Your ma-ma-ma-ma-majesty. How nice to see you looking so well. What a handsome frown you have.

King Bob: Knock it off, Hipp. You've been very hypocritical, and you know what that means.

Voices 1, 2, 3, 4, and 5: Let him have it, your highness.

Mr. Hipp: *(Quickly tucks in his shirt and kneels in front of King Bob.)* Please, your majesty, I am a contrite and broken Hipp. Can you ever forgive me?

Narrator: But the King was very stern with the young man.

Voice 3: Did the King put Mr. Hipp in prison?

Voice 4: Was Mr. Hipp banished from the kingdom for life?

Voice 1: Did the King throw Mr. Hipp out of joint?

(Voices 2, 3, 4, and 5, King Bob and the Narrator all roll their eyes at Voice 1.)

Narrator: Not quite. The King made Mr. Hipp apologize.

King Bob: *(Speaks to Mr. Hipp while pointing at the others.)* Tell them you're sorry.

Mr. Hipp: *(Still on his knees, he turns to face the Voices.)* I'm sorry. It won't happen again.

Voices 1, 2, 3, 4, and 5: That's OK. We understand.

King Bob: Young man, don't ever pretend to be something you aren't, even if you think you can get something out of it.

Mr. Hipp: *(Still kneeling)* Yes, your Bob-ness.

Narrator: From that moment on, Mr. Hipp was a new man.

Mr. Hipp: *(Standing)* My hypocritical days are over. From now on I'll quit pretending to be someone I'm not. Instead I will try to be the best person I can be. I'll give up all my bad habits and start living the way I've been pretending to live.

Voices 1, 2, 3, 4, and 5: Good for you, Mr. Hipp. That's just the way Jesus would want it.

Mr. Hipp: *(To the Voices)* Please, call me Arya.

King Bob: *(Looks puzzled.)* Arya Hipp?

Mr. Hipp: *(Winks at King Bob.)* You bet I am.

Voices 1, 2, 3, 4, and 5: That's awful.

Mr. Hipp: Sorry.

Narrator: And Mr. Hipp was a hypocrite no more.

Voices 1, 2, 3, 4, and 5: Attaboy, Arya.

Narrator: The tale now being told, it is worthy to tell you that Arya Hipp lived happily ever after.

◆◆◆ Discussion Activity ◆◆◆

On a large sheet of newsprint, write the word "hypocrisy" in large letters. Ask:
- **Based on the skit, how do you define the word hypocrisy?**
- **In what ways do we see hypocrisy in everyday life?**
- **In what ways are we sometimes hypocrites?**

Read Matthew 7:3-5 aloud and say: **In this passage, the word *plank* refers to our faults, which we often overlook when we criticize someone else. Jesus stresses that our own faults are often larger than those of others.** Ask:
- **What sort of *planks* might we have in our own eyes?** (List the responses on newsprint.)

- How can we get rid of our own *planks?*
- Why is it important to worry about ourselves before criticizing others?

Say: In the skit, Mr. Hipp becomes a new man when he decides to stop being hypocritical. Ask:

- Is this really possible? Explain why or why not?
- What are some ways we can avoid being hypocritical in our own lives?

The Guy With Coach Tribblewhistle's Nose

Scripture: Luke 15:1-7 and John 3:16

Topic: Popularity

Setting: This scene takes place either in a hallway at school or at the mall.

Props: For Hank, you'll need a fake nose, glasses, a mustache, a floppy hat, and a shirt that is too big for him. The other characters dress as they would for school or for shopping.

Characters:
> **David**—a teenage boy
> **Hank**—a teenage boy trying to change his identity
> **Kim**—a teenage girl

◆◆◆ Script ◆◆◆

David: *(He and Hank bump into each other.)* Whoa, sorry. I didn't see… *(Recognizes his friend.)* Hank?

Hank: *(Keeping his head down)* No, I'm not Hank. You must have me confused with someone else. Hank is home, sick. I mean Hank moved far away. He lives in Switzerland now.

David: Then who are you?

Hank: I'm a new student, very popular. You all are going to love me here.

David: *(Looks more closely.)* Hank, it *is* you. What's with the get-up? And that mustache…what's going on?

Hank: *(Gives up reluctantly.)* Oh, I don't know. It seemed like a good idea at the time.

David: At what time? Halloween?

Hank: Give me a break, will you? I just thought I'd try being someone else for a change—someone different.

David: I'm thinking someone a little *too* different. You look like a tragic accident at a costume party. But why?

Hank: Because I'm tired of being just Hank. I thought maybe if I could be someone else for a while, I could get off to a better start. Most people don't even know I exist. Did you know that Marsha Smith nearly knocked me over today in the hall? She was so busy talking to her friends that she never even saw me. It's like I'm the invisible nerd.

David: *(Looks around suspiciously.)* Is there a hidden camera somewhere?

Hank: No. I'm serious.

David: Look, will you lose the disguise? It's hard to take you seriously when you look like Coach Tribblewhistle with facial hair.

Hank: Coach Tribblewhistle? the gym coach? I don't look that bad, do I?

David: As a matter of fact, you do look that bad.

Hank: *(Takes off the glasses and mustache.)* The mustache *was* tickling my nose anyway.

David: That's better. So what's the big deal. Just because Marsha Smith can't walk and talk at the same time doesn't mean you have to become a mutant power turtle or whatever.

Hank: It's more than that. If this school had social radar, I'd be flying under it.

Kim: *(Walks up from behind Hank. She doesn't recognize him at first.)* Hey, David, who's the new guy. Won't you introduce me?

(Hank winces and ducks his head.)

David: Hi, Kim. No new guys here. Just the same old crowd.

Kim: *(Looks over Hank's shoulder.)* Hank? Is that you? What's with the disguise?

Hank: Argghhh!…

Kim: *(To David)* What's with him?

David: *(To Kim)* This is sort of a guy thing. I'm not sure Hank is in any condition to talk about it right now.

Kim: *(To Hank)* Hey, Hank. You're not trying to pretend you're somebody else just so you can start your life over again, are you?

Hank: Argghhh…

David: *(To Kim)* Amazing! How did you know that?

Kim: Easy. It's also a girl thing.

David: I had no idea.

Kim: Sure. Last year when I ran for class treasurer, I thought I needed to get the most votes to be happy. Then I lost. So I decided I'd start over again by dressing in green and wearing hippie beads. Don't you remember?

David: Oh, yeah. I figured that was the *in* thing.

Kim: No. That was a *Kim* thing. You didn't see anyone else wearing plastic beads, did you?

Hank: *(Takes an interest.)* Did it work? Starting over, I mean.

Kim: No, it didn't. I did get sick of green though.

David: This all reminds me of a discussion we had in youth group a few weeks ago. Somebody asked our sponsors why Jesus seemed to spend more time with the unpopular people in his day than with the popular ones.

Hank: What did the sponsors say?

David: Ms. Johnson said it had more to do with lost sheep than with popularity.

Kim: What does that mean?

David: It means that instead of being impressed by people who had popularity, Jesus came looking for the folks who felt left out. He was like a shepherd who has ninety-nine sheep but still goes looking for the one sheep that's lost.

Hank: Are you saying I'm a lost sheep?

David: I'm saying that sometimes we can all feel lost or lonely, like we're totally on our own. But to God, all of us are important. To God, all of us are popular. Are you familiar with John 3:16?

Hank: "For God so loved the world…" That one?

Kim: "…that he gave his one and only Son…"

David: Right. One thing it means is that no matter how we feel about ourselves, God was willing to let his Son die for us. I figure if God loved *me* enough to do *that*, then I must be pretty special to God.

Hank: OK. You say that I'm important to God. But how does that keep Marsha Smith from knocking me down?

David: It doesn't. But it could help you to get back up.

Hank: Really? How?

Kim: I get it! *(To Hank)* Knowing you are important to God reminds you that he loves you, and that it's worth getting up and trying again. God didn't quit on us, and we shouldn't quit on ourselves.

David: Exactly.

Kim: You know, this popularity thing is tough on everybody. We really need to watch out for each other, too, so that no one feels left out.

David: That's a good point. You never know who's going to feel like a lost sheep. Next time it might be Marsha Smith. Hank, I'm sorry I didn't realize you felt so unnoticed.

Hank: Oh, that's OK.

David: You know, it's not too late to give up being the guy with Coach Tribblewhistle's nose.

Hank: Good point. *(Puts glasses back on.)* I appreciate what both of you have done. You've helped a lot. But I have one more favor to ask.

Kim: What is it?

Hank: Would you help me sneak out of here?

Kim: Sneak out? Why?

David: Haven't you heard anything we've said? You *don't need* to hide.

Hank: Are you kidding? Dressed this way? I've got to get home and change before somebody sees me!

◆◆◆ Discussion Activity ◆◆◆

(A big part of growing up involves coming to terms with who we are and discovering our strengths and talents. Many young people will, from time to time, share Hank's feelings of inadequacy.)

Form two teams for a game of Charades. Give one team words such as "lonely, lost, insecure, unpopular, isolated," and the other team words such as "friends, popular, sincere, comfortable, and outgoing." Have teams take turns acting out their words.

When the game is finished, ask:

● **What were some of your thoughts about the words your team was given?**

● **Share some times when you felt lonely, lost, insecure, unpopular, or isolated.**

Read Luke 15:1-7 aloud to the group. Ask:

● **What does Luke mean by lost sheep?**

● **Who is the shepherd who goes in search of the lost sheep?**

● **Why do you think he leaves all the other sheep to look for just one lost sheep?**

A Place in This World

Scripture: 1 Corinthians 12:12-24

Topic: Self-esteem

Setting: A birthday party

Props: You'll need a table containing party items, including napkins, in the middle of the stage. (You might also want to put up other party decorations.) Several chairs should be located around the room, with one of them at stage right in the far corner. Michael W. Smith's "A Place in This World" may be played as background music and stopped periodically. You will need a tape player so that the *thoughts* can be played. The tape player may also be used to record the sound of a doorbell. April carries a purse with one Bible promise book in it. Additionally, you'll need a Bible promise book as a gift for Misty.

Characters:
> **Misty**—a popular teen
> **Eric**—an average teen
> **Jeremy**—an unpopular teen
> **Mark**—a shy Christian teen
> **April**—a Christian teen
> Several other teenagers as the party guests

◆◆◆ Script ◆◆◆

(Characters move about as if they are attending a party. Several groups of about three teenagers each gather around the room. The doorbell rings and Misty answers brightly.)

Misty: Hi, Jeremy! Come on in!

Jeremy: *(Dejected)* Hi, Misty. Happy birthday. *(He moves toward the refreshment table as his voice is heard on tape.)*

Jeremy's thoughts: Why was I invited? No one wants me around. The only ones who ever talk to me are Misty and April. *(He sits in the chair at stage right and begins tearing a napkin. He tears it slowly and deliberately, and alternates his attention between the napkin and the other people in the room. It appears by his actions that he prefers to be alone, yet he also gazes longingly at the others. The doorbell rings again and Misty answers.)*

Misty: *(Brightly)* Mark! So glad you could make it. I thought your youth group had band practice or something?

Mark: *(Is clearly uncomfortable)* Ah, well, practice ended early, so I just came anyway. I hope that's OK?

Mark's thoughts: What if Misty thinks being in a church youth group band is weird or something?

Misty: Of course it's OK! Come on in! *(She motions for Mark to join the others.)*

Mark's thoughts: Whew. She didn't say anything else about the band. Good.

(He joins a group as the doorbell rings again. Misty turns to face the door. Eric enters.)

Misty: *(Brightly)* Hi, Eric! Come on in!

Eric: *(Smiling)* Thanks, Misty. *(Surveys the room.)* Great party, huh? It sure is cool your parents did all this for you. I hear they even called the school to make sure they had everyone's name.

Misty: Yeah, my parents are something, all right. *(She shakes her head skeptically.)*

Misty's thoughts: They didn't even ask me what I wanted to do for my birthday. All I wanted was a simple birthday dinner. I didn't want the whole school over for a party. I get tired of trying to please everyone.

(Misty and Eric cross the room to a group. Misty joins Jeremy.)

Misty: *(Concerned)* Jeremy? You OK?

Jeremy's thoughts: *(Panicked)* Why is she asking me that? Don't I look OK? Now, how do I answer her?

Jeremy: *(Depressed)* Yeah, I'm fine.

Misty's thoughts: All he ever does is mope.

Misty: Well, have fun, OK?

(Jeremy nods as Misty moves off to answer the doorbell.)

Misty: *(Brightly)* April! Hi! Come on in.

Misty's thoughts: *(Puzzled)* I thought Christians didn't attend parties, but Mark's here and now April. Could I be wrong? Gee, I hope I didn't act *too* surprised.

April: I'm not too late, am I?

Misty: No, not at all.

April: Happy birthday, Misty. Here, I brought you something. *(Hands Misty a Bible promise book.)*

Misty: A Bible promise book? *(Begins flipping curiously through the book.)*

April's thoughts: Yes, Misty. We all need God's promises. Sometimes we try so hard to please others, we forget we only need to please God.

April: *(Grinning)* I think everyone needs one—right next to their Bible.

Mark: *(Sees April.)* Hey, April!

Mark's thoughts: I'm glad she's here. She always knows what to say.

April: Hi, Mark! Practice ended early, huh?

April's thoughts: I wish Mark had more confidence in himself.

Misty: Let's join the others, OK?

(She closes the promise book as they walk toward the others.)

Mark and April's thoughts: *(In unison)* Poor Misty. She tries so hard to fit in with everyone.

Eric: Hey, April! How's it going?

April: Awesome. You?

Eric's thoughts: Me? I'm the average guy, remember? How do you think it's going?

Eric: OK, I guess. *(To Misty, curiously)* Say, Misty, what's that? *(Points to the Bible promise book.)*

Misty: *(Embarrassed)* Uh, a present from April.

Eric's thoughts: I didn't know we were supposed to bring presents! Man! Why didn't I think about a present? Why do I *always* mess up? Just for once, I wish I could get *something* right!

April: It's a Bible promise book.

Mark's thoughts: Now, why didn't I think of that?

(Jeremy looks up, interested. Crosses over to the crowd forming around April, Mark, Eric, and Misty.)

Jeremy: *(Puzzled)* A what?

(All turn to stare at him, surprised.)

Jeremy's thoughts: I never get presents. Not even from my parents.

April: Oh! I almost forgot. I brought you one, too, Jeremy. *(Digs in purse, produces second book, and give it to Jeremy.)*

Jeremy: *(Astonished)* You did? Why?

Eric: *(To Jeremy, curiously)* Can I see that?

Jeremy's thoughts: *(Incredulous)* He's talking to me?

Jeremy: I guess so. *(Hands over the book.)*

Eric: What's it for?

April: It helps you look up Scriptures when you have a question or a problem.

Misty: What kind of problem or question?

Misty's thoughts: Fear?

Jeremy's thoughts: Loneliness?

Eric's thoughts: Worry?

Mark's thoughts: Courage.

April's thoughts: Faith.

Mark: *(Firmly)* Anything. The Bible has answers for any situation, but first, you have to ask Jesus Christ into your heart.

Mark's thoughts: Hey! I can't believe I said that! Wow!

April's thoughts: Way to go, Mark!

Eric: *(Shaking his head)* You can't make me believe that one little book has the answer to every problem. I know lots of Christians who have problems, too.

April: *(Firmly)* The Bible does have the answers, but sometimes we have a hard time finding them and believing them. Christians aren't perfect, you know.

Mark: No, we're not perfect, but Jesus will help us when we ask, and we can help each other. That's why the Bible calls us the body of Christ. We all have a place in that body, too.

Mark's thoughts: *(Excited)* I can't believe I'm doing this! This is neat!

Jeremy: *(Curiously)* Do you really think so? Well, I've tried everything else. I might as well try this. But, I'm not sure where I'd belong. I'm not sure what I would have to change if I became a Christian so I could fit in someplace.

April: Jeremy, you don't need to change to fit in.

(Others nod as she pauses.)

April's thoughts: How do I say this, God?

Mark: Jeremy, God has a place in this world for everyone. There are even Bible verses that say so.

April's thoughts: Thank you, God!

Jeremy: There are? Can I see them?

Everyone: We want to see them, too!

Misty: Wait! I think I have a Bible in my room. *(She runs offstage.)*

◆◆◆ Discussion Activity ◆◆◆

Read 1 Corinthians 12:12-24 aloud, particularly emphasizing verses 15 and 16. Pause after reading verse 17, and ask: **What point do you think God was trying to make here?**

Continue reading and pause after verse 19. Ask: **Why do you think God is stressing the importance of being different?**

Continue reading until you finish the passage and then ask:
- **Why do you think God made us each different?**
- **What special talents and unique characteristics did God give you?**

Not the Place for Me

Scripture: Proverbs 15:28-30

Topic: Gossip and Following God's Will

Setting: This scene takes place during the coffee hour between worship services at Lizzy's church, where she's brought Joel for the first time.

Props: A few people should be holding coffee cups, and two or three of them should have Bibles. Scatter a few chairs around the stage so church members can either stand or sit.

Characters:

Joel—an unchurched teenager who is attending church for the first time

Lizzy—Joel's girlfriend, whose church they are attending

Mrs. Thornberry—the church busybody who acts overly polite when she's really being rude

Pastor Carver—the youth pastor who the kids like

Ann—a girl from the youth group who is gossipy and opinionated

Lexie—a new Christian who is outgoing

Sasha—a girl from the youth group who is insecure but sincere

Tony—a guy from the youth group who is nice and who enjoys being out-numbered by the girls

Church Members—as many or as few as desired

◆◆◆ Script ◆◆◆

(As Joel and Lizzy walk into the room, all of the other cast members are in little groups talking and laughing. The adult church members are dressed up, while the youth group kids are more casual. Joel is in jeans.)

Joel: *(Stops at the edge of the room.)* Lizzy, I'm not sure I want to do this.

Lizzy: *(Tries to pull him into the room, teasingly.)* Why not? It's just church. Besides, I want you to meet my friends.

Joel: *(Pulls away.)* I've never been to a church before.

Lizzy: It's no big deal. I mean the God part is, but being here isn't. I've gone to this church my whole life.

Joel: That's what I mean. I don't even know how to act.

Lizzy: Just be yourself. You're yourself with me, and I like you. *(Puts her arm around him.)*

Joel: But what if I do something wrong or say something stupid?

Lizzy: Nobody cares. They'll just be glad you came.

Joel: *(Sighs.)* OK.

Lizzy: Good! Now come on. *(Takes his hand and leads him across the room.)*

Mrs. Thornberry: *(Stopping them before they can get to Lizzy's friends.)* Well, hello, Lizzy! It's so good to see you!

Lizzy: *(Anxious to keep moving, but not wanting to be rude)* Thanks.

Mrs. Thornberry: How is that brother of yours, anyway? I've noticed he hasn't been to church for the last few weeks. I hope he hasn't turned his back on the Lord.

Lizzy: Oh no, nothing like that.

Mrs. Thornberry: I'm certainly relieved to hear that. I actually thought it might be because of that little acne problem he has. A touch difficult to show that face in public, isn't it?

Lizzy: No, his face is just fine. *(Pulls Joel away a step.)* We've got to go…

Mrs. Thornberry: *(Stops Lizzy.)* Not before you introduce me to this nice young man.

Lizzy: *(Rolls her eyes.)* Mrs. Thornberry, this is Joel. Joel, this is Mrs. Thornberry.

Mrs. Thornberry: Lovely to meet you. I don't think I've seen you here before.

Joel: This is my first time.

Mrs. Thornberry: Well, welcome! How do you like it so far? I mean, compared to your home church.

Joel: I don't actually go to a church.

Mrs. Thornberry: Oh, well then it's a good thing you're here, isn't it?

Joel: Um, yeah. I guess.

Mrs. Thornberry: Lizzy, do your parents realize he's not "one of us"?

Lizzy: Yes. We really need to get going…

Mrs. Thornberry: Of course you do, but *(confidentially)* you might want to let your young man know that although many of you teenagers wear blue jeans, it really isn't appropriate.

Lizzy: Joel looks just fine. *(Pulls Joel away.)*

Joel: That's it. I'm outta here! *(Heads toward the door.)*

Lizzy: I'm sorry! She's just like that. She didn't mean anything.

Joel: It doesn't matter. I don't want to do this.

Lizzy: Wait, Joel. I'll go with you.

Pastor Carver: *(Intercepts them before they get out the door.)* Lizzy! Wait up!

Lizzy: Hi, Pastor Carver. We were just leaving.

Pastor Carver: Then I'm glad I caught you. I didn't see you at the first service.

Joel: *(Somewhat hostile)* We weren't there.

Pastor Carver: No matter. I just wanted to say welcome.

Lizzy: Mrs. Thornberry cornered us on the way in.

Pastor Carver: *(Apologetically)* Yeah, I saw that. My apologies. I'm afraid she's one of those people God uses to remind me to love my neighbor—no matter what!

(That gets a small smile from Joel.)

Lizzy: This is my boyfriend, Joel.

Pastor Carver: Good to meet you. I'm Pastor Carver, the youth pastor around here. Guess that makes me the oldest kid in the room!

Joel: *(More friendly)* Hi.

Pastor Carver: Sorry you're not staying for the second service. They've lost their minds, and they're letting me preach this week! You might say I have a slightly unique style.

Lizzy: We really can't stay, but…

Joel: *(Hesitantly)* Actually, I guess we could.

Lizzy: Really?

Joel: Yeah.

Pastor Carver: I think you'll find that there are only a few Mrs. Thornberry-types. The rest of us are pretty normal.

Joel: *(Relaxing and joking a little)* Like you?

Pastor Carver: *(Laughing)* Well, I wouldn't go so far as to call me normal…

Lizzy: Me neither! Thanks, Pastor Carver. *(To Joel)* Let's go meet my friends.

(They move over to Lizzy's friends.)

Ann: Lizzy!

Lexie: And this must be the famous Joel! We've heard so much about you!

Lizzy: *(Trying to get them not to say too much)* Not *that* much!

Tony: You're just the only thing she ever talks about. I'm Tony.

Joel: Hi.

Lizzy: He got to meet Mrs. Thornberry. *(Everyone moans.)*

Sasha: You poor thing!

Joel: Yeah! And I met that Pastor Carver guy. He seems OK.

Tony: He's the best.

Sasha: Yeah, we love Carv.

Lexie: Lizzy said you've never been to church before.

Joel: *(Defensive)* So what?

Lexie: Nothing. It's just good that you came. I just started coming here last Christmas.

Ann: With me!

Tony: I'm glad there's another guy around. We men are always outnumbered!

(Girls all start fawning over him, "It's so tough," "You must hate all that attention," "Poor Tony," and so forth.)

Joel: Looks like you have it pretty rough. Glad I can help.

Lizzy: *(Puts her arm around Joel.)* Don't be too glad. You're not going to be much help.

Ann: Not if Shelly has anything to say about it.

Lizzy: *(Flatly)* She doesn't.

Joel: Who's Shelly?

Sasha: *(Emphasizes each word, imitating the type.)* Just the most perfect, prissy, all-over-any-man-in-the-room, perky, cheerleader type in the world.

Lizzy: *(Flatly)* She's nobody.

Sasha: *(Innocently)* Isn't that what I said?

Tony: They're just jealous because she's so…

Ann: Sleazy.

Lexie: And no, we are not jealous.

Sasha: We just hate her.

Tony: You guys shouldn't be so hard on her. She's nice.

Ann: *(Pretends to hang all over Tony.)* I bet she is.

Lexie: *(Hangs on to Tony, too.)* If you're a member of the male species.

Sasha: Be glad she's not here, Lizzy.

Lizzy: *(Squeezes Joel.)* Trust me. I am!

Lexie: You'd have to watch out for Joel if she was. *(Pretends to be Shelly, overexaggerating how she would be interested in Joel.)* Oh, Joel, you're so cute! Don't you just want to dump Lizzy and be with me?

(Everyone laughs except Joel.)

Sasha: *(Excited about the gossip.)* Did you hear what her dad did at the church board meeting?

Tom: Yeah! Can you believe it?

Ann: *(Crosses her arms.)* Well, Mrs. Barnes really did have it coming.

Lexie: You're taking *his* side?

Ann: *(Puts her hands on her hips.)* No, I just think that she's already got so much power. It's about time someone put her in her place.

Tony: That sounds like your dad talking.

Ann: *(With superiority)* Well, my dad *was* there. You only heard the rumor.

(Joel starts to back away from the group.)

Lizzy: Where are you going?

Joel: *(Pushes Lizzy's arm off gently.)* I'm gonna go.

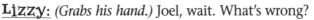

Lizzy: *(Grabs his hand.)* Joel, wait. What's wrong?

Joel: *(Lowers his voice and pulls his hand away.)* I don't want to talk about it here.

Lizzy: I don't understand.

Joel: *(Crosses his arms in discomfort.)* I thought you church people were supposed to be different.

Lizzy: Different from what?

Joel: From everybody. But you're not. Your friends are just like the kids at school.

Lizzy: So?

Joel: So I thought they'd be nicer. More like God, or whatever.

Lizzy: *(Takes it too lightly.)* They are. They were just joking about Shelly. And you should have heard what happened at that meeting!

Joel: I don't want to. What's the point of coming here if it's just the same as everywhere else?

Lexie: *(Overhears and comes over to Joel and Lizzy.)* It's not, Joel. *(Embarrassed)* It's not supposed to be anyway.

Ann: *(Joins them and looks apologetic.)* Sometimes we just get carried away.

Joel: Look, I'm not trying to act like I'm better than you, but I thought *you* were supposed to be better than everyone else.

Lizzy: No, we're not. I didn't mean to make it seem like that.

Joel: Then why do you get up early on Sundays?

Tony: *(Joins them.)* Because it's about God.

Joel: What is?

Lexie: *(Joins them with Sasha.)* We really messed this up. I'm sorry.

Joel: Is *sorry* supposed to make it better?

Sasha: *(Considers for a minute.)* Yeah, it actually is. Not just saying it, but meaning it! When I first came here, I didn't know anything about forgiveness.

Joel: Forgiveness?

Sasha: It's what happens when we tell God we're sorry and really mean it. He forgives us.

Joel: For what?

Tony: For everything. All the stupid, mean, dumb stuff we do all the time.

Lexie: *(Regretfully)* Like making fun of Shelly.

Sasha: *(With guilt)* And hating her.

Ann: *(Apologetic)* And talking about other people in the church.

Joel: Do you think God cares about that stuff?

Lizzy: He cares about everything.

Joel: Then how come you still act like everyone else in the world?

Lizzy: Because we're human.

Tony: And stupid.

Sasha: But God knows we're going to mess up and loves us anyway.

Lizzy: That's why we come here.

Ann: It's about letting God get closer to you so he can show you how much he loves you.

Joel: *(Skeptical)* God loves me?

Lizzy: *(Puts her arms around Joel.)* More than I love you. He loves us all that much.

Tony: Hopefully we'll pay enough attention to him to realize it. And maybe that'll help us not mess up so much.

Lexie: But if we do, he still loves us.

Joel: I'm not sure I get it.

Sasha: None of us totally gets it. That's another reason we come here—to learn a little more about it.

Pastor Carver: *(Comes over to the group and puts his hand on Tony's shoulder.)* We're about to start. You guys better make sure you get a good seat for this one!

(Everyone is quiet and looking at Joel.)

Pastor Carver: *(Not realizing what's going on)* Come on, you don't want to miss this once-in-a-lifetime chance!

Joel: *(Pauses.)* You're right. Let's go. *(Puts his arm around Lizzy.)*

(Everyone else smiles as they walk toward the sanctuary. Pastor Carver watches them, shakes his head, and then follows.)

◆◆◆ Discussion Activity ◆◆◆

Say: Joel didn't understand why the kids were making fun of Shelly or why Mrs. Thornberry was so rude. He had different expectations for people who call themselves "Christians." Ask:

- Why do people expect Christians to act differently?
- What do Christians sometimes say about themselves when they get caught acting "just like everybody else"?
- If Christians really are different, how do they get that way?
- How should we make being "in the world but not of the world" a priority?

Read Proverbs 15: 28-30, then ask:

- In what ways does God call us to be obedient?
- What good comes from following God's will?
- What bad comes from ignoring his instruction?

Nobody's Supposed to Know

Scripture: 1 Corinthians 3:16-17

Topic: Drug and Alcohol Abuse

Setting: Casey's house, where she is hosting some church friends

Props: For this scene, you will need some furniture arranged like a living room (several folding chairs in a row will be adequate to make a couch). Scatter a few magazines and pillows around. Provide Dad with a bottle of some kind, and the kids with back packs, book bags, notebooks, pens, and so forth. You will also need a door chime or similar sound.

Characters:

Casey—a teenage girl who is trying to face her parents' problem alone
Mom—Casey's mother who gets mean when she's been drinking or doing drugs
Dad—Casey's father who starts acting silly when he's been drinking or doing drugs
Joe—Casey's friend who is smart and fun loving
Tom—Casey's friend who is kind and sensitive
Abby—Casey's friend who is social and outgoing
Sonia—Casey's friend who is a creative problem-solver
Doorbell Ringer—someone to ring a bell when the doorbell rings

◆◆◆ Script ◆◆◆

(Casey tidies her living room—straightening pillows, putting away magazines, and so forth.)

Mom: *(Enters drunk, although not obviously so. There is, however, something odd about her behavior.)* What are you doing?

Casey: *(Guiltily stops cleaning.)* Um, nothing, Mom. Just picking up a little.

Mom: *(Grabs one of the pillows.)* Why? Don't you think I keep the house neat enough? Am I too messy for you?

Casey: *(Laughing nervously)* No, of course not. It's just that I made a mess. I didn't want you to have any extra work.

Mom: Oh, so now you think I'm lazy!

Casey: No, Mom! Really. Look, the truth is I have some friends coming over. We're going to plan an overnight at Abby's church.

Mom: So Casey has friends! *(Laughs.)* I didn't think you had any friends. Why haven't I met them?

Casey: You did…I, um, have to get some stuff together. *(Tries to leave.)* I'll be in my room.

Mom: *(Throws pillow down.)* You're not going anywhere! I want to know why you haven't had your friends over before.

Casey: I just haven't. We hang out at church and the mall and stuff.

Mom: Maybe you just don't want them to see your dear, sweet mother. Maybe you're embarrassed by her!

Casey: *(Picks up the pillow and puts in on a chair.)* No, Mom, I'm not. Really!

Mom: *(Yelling)* Yes you are! That's why you don't look at me when you talk. That's why you never bring your friends here. That's why…

Dad: *(Walks in carrying a bottle. He is drunk too.)* Hey, what's all the yelling about?

Casey: Nothing, Daddy.

Mom: Nothing? She's having some of her little friends over. Did you know she even had little friends?

Dad: Good for you! *(Takes a drink.)*

Mom: No! She's hiding things from us. *(Gets weepy.)* She shouldn't hide things from us. We love her and want her to tell us everything. Right? Where did we go wrong?

Dad: *(Hands Mom the bottle.)* Here, have a little drink. It's OK. Her little friends are coming over now. Isn't that right?

Casey: Yes.

Dad: Good. We'll meet them when they get here, right?

Casey: Yeah.

Dad: We'll go on upstairs, have a drink, and wait for them to come. OK?

Mom: But you tell us when they're here!

Casey: Sure, Mom.

(Mom and Dad exit.)

Casey: *(Kneels in prayer.)* Dear God, please help me get through this. I didn't want my friends to come over in the first place, and now Mom and Dad are going to wreck everything! Please don't let them come down while my friends are here. Let them pass out first. God, I couldn't take it if anyone found out! Or maybe you could make them sober really quick. Just this once, God. Please! I know you're going to help me make them better. Once you've healed them, then my friends can be over whenever I want. Please just let this work out.

(Doorbell rings.)

Casey: Please, God! Amen.

(Casey goes to the door and lets her friends in. They say, "hi," "nice place," "how's it going," and so forth as they come in. They all sit down, open their backpacks, and take out paper and pens. Casey keeps looking nervously toward the door through which her parents exited.)

Abby: We've got to make this the best lock-in ever! Pastor Mike said it was up to us to plan something even better than last summer.

Tom: It'll be hard to beat.

Joe: That was so fun!

Sonia: I had this idea for a mini-golf course.

Joe: Inside the church?

Sonia: Not in the sanctuary or anything, but in the hallways and stuff. We'd use paper cups for the holes and brooms for the golf clubs.

Abby: That could be really fun! What do you think, Casey?

Casey: *(Distracted)* What? Oh, sure, anything's fine.

Tom: Are you OK?

Casey: *(Pretending to be excited)* Sure. You said golf in the sanctuary, right?

Abby: Not quite. What's up?

Casey: Nothing. I'm just tired or something.

Sonia: *(Not looking convinced)* OK. Well, I was thinking that since there's all that old furniture stored in the basement, we could end the course there.

Joe: Going down the stairs could be tricky.

Tom: We could make it even harder if we added tubes or something that you had to send the ball down.

Abby: What if we block off the bottom part…

(Dad and Mom enter, much more obviously drunk this time. Abby, Tom, Joe, and Sonia are confused by their behavior and embarrassed for Casey. Casey is humiliated and scared.)

Dad: See, I told you I heard the door. Ding, dong! *(Laughs.)*

Mom: Oh, you did bring your little friends over. That's so wonderful! Casey tells me you're planning a little party thing.

Casey: *(Jumps up.)* Yeah, we are. Why don't you give us some time, and I'll tell you all about it later.

Mom: No, no, no! I want to hear all about it now. *(Drops down on a chair near Sonia and touches her hair.)* Look at how pretty she is. Casey, you didn't tell me you had pretty friends.

Dad: Would anybody like something to drink?

Tom: *(Uncomfortably)* Sure.

Abby: *(Tries to be polite.)* Yeah, thanks.

Dad: Good! You want that straight up or on the rocks?

Casey: *(Starts to panic.)* Very funny, Dad. Of course we want it on the rocks. Soda's no good without ice.

Dad: Soda? Oh yeah, we could have some of that too!

Mom: I used to be pretty. Pretty! Pretty! Your friends are pretty, Casey. Oops! Not the boys, though. Boys aren't supposed to be pretty, are they?

Casey: You are pretty, Mom. *(Pulls Mom up.)* Why don't you go upstairs and put on some makeup. Then you'll be really pretty.

Dad: Upstairs? Good idea. *(To Joe)* Know why?

Joe: Um, no.

Dad: Because I've got something yummy up there.

Casey: *(Guides Mom toward the exit.)* Go on up, then. Please.

Dad: But your friends might like some…some…stuff. Yeah, I scored some righteous stuff from this dude at work. Isn't that how you kids say it?

Casey: Yes, Dad, but we're kind of busy. Maybe later.

Dad: Oh! OK then. Mommy will come with me, won't you? *(Leads Mom out of the room.)*

Mom: I used to be pretty.

(Casey sits down and covers her face. Everyone is quiet for a minute.)

Tom: Casey?

Casey: I think you should go now.

Abby: *(Moves to where Casey is sitting.)* I think we should stay.

Casey: It's no big deal. Why don't you just plan the lock-in without me.

Tom: We're your friends.

Sonia: We want to help.

Casey: *(Pretends to be fine.)* Help with what? They were just goofing around.

Joe: Come on, that was for real.

Casey: You weren't supposed to find out. Nobody was.

Abby: How long have they been…like this?

Casey: Awhile.

Tom: Is that why you haven't been coming to church much lately?

Casey: Yeah.

Sonia: It seems pretty serious.

Casey: It wasn't so bad at first. I mean, they just had friends over for drinks and stuff. But they started drinking a lot when no one was here. And then my dad made this new friend at work…

Tom: This is so weird. I mean, my parents are the ones telling me not to take drugs or drink.

Sonia: Tom!

Casey: No, he's right. It's all backward.

Abby: You don't do that, do you?

Casey: No! I don't ever want to be like that. They keep telling me everything's fine, they can handle it. But I'm not so sure. The electricity got turned off because they forgot to pay the bills again. Sometimes they're gone for a few days, and I don't know where they are.

Joe: What are you going to do?

Casey: I've been praying about it. I know God will heal them. He'll make them stop. I just don't get why he hasn't yet.

Tom: I don't think God works like that.

Casey: Then what's the point of praying?

Abby: God brought *us* here, didn't he?

Sonia: Maybe we're supposed to be here.

Joe: Yeah. We can help.

Casey: How?

Sonia: We've got to tell someone.

Casey: No! You have to swear you won't tell anyone.

Tom: You can't do this alone.

Joe: We could talk to Pastor Mike.

Casey: No. They'll get in trouble. God will fix it.

Abby: God's not just going to wave a magic wand, Casey.

Sonia: What if they don't come home one of these times?

Casey: Don't say that!

Joe: It's true. They're in this deep.

Casey: But I'm scared.

Tom: We'll be here for you.

Abby: We promise.

Casey: They'll hate me.

Sonia: Maybe at first. But they'll understand when they're better.

Casey: Pastor Mike will think I'm some kind of terrible person.

Joe: No, he won't. He cares about you.

Abby: We all do.

Sonia: He said he'd be at the church all afternoon in case we had questions about the lock-in. Let's go over and talk to him.

Casey: Now?

Tom: Yeah.

Casey: I'm so scared.

Joe: You want to pray before we go?

Casey: Yes.

(They all hold hands and bow their heads.)

Abby: Dear God, please help us do the right thing.

Tom: Help Casey not to be scared.

Joe: Let Pastor Mike know what to do.

Sonia: Give Casey the strength to do this.

Casey: Please help my parents.

All: Amen.

(They all get their stuff and start to go. Just before they leave, Casey looks back to where her parents exited. Then they all walk out.)

◆◆◆ Discussion Activity ◆◆◆

Before the meeting, draw the outline of someone on a large piece of paper. Be sure to leave enough room on either side of the drawing to write a few words. On the left side of the drawing, write "God's Temple." On the right side of the drawing, write "Drinking" and "Drugs." Hang it on a wall.

Read 1 Corinthians 3:16-17 aloud and ask: **What parts of "God's temple" can we use to serve God?** (Kids may give responses such as "a brain to gain knowledge," "eyes to see those in need," "ears to listen to people," and so forth.) Write their responses on the left side next to the appropriate body part. Ask:

● **What does using drugs and alcohol do to each of these parts?** (Teenagers may give responses such as "makes it hard to think," "can't see things clearly," "difficult to listen to good advice people give you," and so forth.)

● **In what ways can using drugs and alcohol bring honor to God's temple?**

● **What does God say will happen to a temple that is not properly used?**

● **How can a person's body be destroyed using drugs and alcohol?**

● **What consequences do drugs and alcohol have on families? on friends? on finances?**

● **What can you do to help a friend who is using drugs or alcohol?**

Gossip of the Century

Scripture: James 3:5 and Ephesians 4:29

Topic: Gossip

Setting: The scene takes place during lunch time at school.

Props: Place a table at center stage. Leave the back center stage open for the crowd to gather. In addition, you will need two or three lunch trays, a crown, a certificate with "Gossip of the Century" typed on it, a red or purple robe, a statuette, and some plastic or real red roses. You'll need a tape player for the recorded voices.

Characters:
Amber—the gossip
Shannon—a helpful friend
Ben—a teenager
Michael—a teenager
Ryan—a teenager
Crystal—a teenager
Linda—a teenager
Three or four more teenagers

◆◆◆ Script ◆◆◆

(Amber and Shannon sit at the table with lunch trays. Michael, Crystal, Ben, Ryan, and Linda remain offstage. Other teens gather together back center stage.)

Amber: *(Says in a whisper.)* Shannon, did you hear about Ben?

Shannon: *(Shakes her head.)* No, but I really don't want to know. I don't like gossip.

Amber: Oh, but it's true! You see… *(Leans over and whispers in Shannon's ear.)*

Shannon: *(Sighing)* You know, Amber, one day you'll get into a lot of trouble gossiping. You're probably the gossip of the century!

Amber: *(Offended)* It's not gossip; it's the truth!

Shannon: *(Stands and picks up a tray.)* Gossip doesn't have to be a lie. Why should I care what Ryan said that Crystal said that Linda said that Ben did?

Amber: Well, I thought you might want to pray for him. You're always talking about praying for people.

Shannon: *(Sadly)* I can pray for Ben without the details, you know. And you could have prayed for him instead of telling me. *(She leaves.)*

Amber: *(Says to the audience)* Well, I'm not gossiping! I'm not! *(She pushes her tray to the side and lays her head down briefly on the table. Raising her head, she sees Michael entering and waves him over.)* Hey, Michael!

Michael: *(Wearily)* Yeah, Amber, whaddya want?

Amber: *(Eagerly)* Did you hear about Ben? He…

Michael: *(Interrupting)* I'm tired of it, Amber. You and your gossip. Get a grip! *(Michael stomps off to join the crowd back center stage. Amber watches in disbelief. She turns to see Crystal entering.)*

Amber: Crystal! *(Crystal approaches Amber reluctantly.)* Did you see what Michael just did to me?

Crystal: What did you say about him?

Amber: *(Defensively)* Nothing! I promise!

Crystal: *You* promise? I remember the last time you made me a promise. The entire school knew about it before the end of the day. I was never so embarrassed in my entire life.

Amber: *(Hesitantly)* But…I…well, I said I was sorry!

Crystal: *(Sarcastically)* Oh, sure. That really helps, huh? I'll never believe anything you say again.

Amber: *(Tearfully)* But, this time I mean it.

Crystal: *(Shakes her head.)* Yeah, right.

(Crystal joins the group at back center stage as Ben and Ryan enter together. They point in Amber's direction and begin to talk and laugh.)

Amber: *(Jumps up.)* Ben! Ryan! What are you saying about me?

Ryan: *(Crosses back over to Amber.)* What makes you think we're talking about you?

Ben: *(Follows Ryan and tweaks Amber's hair.)* Yeah, Miss Gossip. Not everyone talks about people the way you do.

Amber: *(Tearfully)* I don't gossip.

Ryan: Yeah, right! We know.

Ben: You just tell the truth, that's all. Right?

(Ryan and Ben laugh and join the group at back center stage. Linda enters and walks directly to Amber. Amber wipes away tears as Linda approaches.)

Linda: What's wrong, Amber?

Amber: I can't believe how mean everyone's being.

Linda: Mean? How?

Amber: *(Grateful to have a seemingly friendly ear)* Oh, you know! Teasing me and everything. Ben called me a gossip.

Linda: Sometimes the truth hurts, doesn't it?

Amber: *(Shocked)* The truth?

Linda: *(Surprised)* Well, sure. Everyone knows you're a gossip.

Amber: I'm not!

Linda: *(Rolls her eyes.)* Oh, please. Remember what you said about me last week?

Amber: *(Weakly)* What?

Linda: See? You can't even remember telling people that I went out with Ben!

Amber: Oh, that. Well, you see, Oscar said so, so I thought…

Linda: You thought, all right. About as much as this lunch table here. You *didn't* think, Amber, you just talked. And now, well, Ben barely talks to me. And I have you to thank.

Amber: *(Sniffling)* I'm sorry, Linda. Really, really sorry.

Linda: *(Smiling)* Well, live and learn. Guess I should forgive you since you asked so nicely, shouldn't I?

Amber: *(Looks hopeful.)* Yes, please.

Linda: Then you're forgiven, I guess. Oh! Hey, everybody, I almost forgot! *(To the crowd back center stage)* Quick, come over here! Amber's won an award!

Amber: *(Brightening)* An award?

Linda: *(Grins.)* Sure thing. You've been chosen *(pauses)* Gossip of the Century! Congratulations!

(Linda presents Amber with a certificate. Ben and Ryan give her the statuette and roses. Crystal presents her with the crown, and Michael places the robe around her shoulders. All students form a circle surrounding Amber, facing inward toward her. They begin to march around her slowly.)

Crowd: *(Chants and repeats several times.)* Gossip! Gossip! Gossip!

Amber: *(Tosses everything off, covers her ears with both hands, and sobs.)* No! No! I'm not!

(She sits down and lays her head on the table in a defeated manner. The crowd slowly disperses one by one, still chanting "Gossip" as they leave. After they exit, Shannon enters.)

Shannon: *(Shakes Amber's shoulder.)* Amber! Amber!

Amber: *(Groggily)* What?

Shannon: Wake up! You'll be late for class!

Amber: Late? Class? You mean *(pauses)*, it was a dream?

Shannon: *(Puzzled)* What was?

Amber: *(Brightening)* Never mind. I'll be there in a sec. *(Pauses.)* And, Shannon?

Shannon: Yeah?

Amber: *(Slowly)* I've been thinking about what you said. I might have a problem with gossip. Just maybe.

Shannon: *(Smiles briefly.)* Keep thinking, Amber. *(She exits, leaving Amber alone onstage.)*

Amber: *(Grins.)* Then again, maybe not!

(Stands up and the certificate falls to the floor. She picks it up and her eyes widen as a voice, played from a tape player, echoes over the entire stage.)

Voice: Gossip of the Century!

(The crowd laughs from offstage as Amber stands still, looking shocked.)

◆◆◆ Discussion Activity ◆◆◆

Divide the participants into small groups. Give each group a pen and some paper, and have each choose a secretary/leader to take notes and to keep the group talking.

Say: **Rather than playing the game of Gossip, we're going to discuss practical ways to keep others from gossiping.** Read James 3:5-6 aloud. Give the groups ten minutes to come up with at least five ways to keep someone from gossiping or to keep from listening to a gossip. After allowing adequate time for discussion, have a member of each group read the solutions they came up with.

Read Ephesians 4:29 aloud, and ask:

● **Why do people gossip?**
● **Why do you think God's word instructs us not to gossip?**
● **Who does gossip hurt more, the one who does the gossiping or the person gossiped about? Why?**

It's No Big Deal

Scripture: Proverbs 14:9 and Romans 6:23

Topic: Consequences and Sin

Setting: The scene takes place in a school gym.

Props: You'll need some towels, folding chairs with school books and bags on them, and some gym mats (if you have access to them). The stage should give the impression of a school gym with a mock wall (preferably painted like brick) on the far right. You'll also need purses for Micah and Allison, a small bag of chips, a pen, and the sound of a school bell for changing classes. In addition, make a sign that reads "Next day."

Characters:
Micah—a teenage girl
Allison—a teenager
Jennifer—a teenager
Amy—a teenager
Sarah—a teenager
Ms. Bailey—the gym teacher
Several other teenage girls

 **◆◆◆ Script ◆◆◆**

(The scene opens with girls dressed in gym shorts and with towels slung across their shoulders. Micah should be dressed a little differently from the others, giving her a more athletic, "tough" look. If you have mats, they should be placed stage left. The girls gather their school books from the folding chairs arranged center stage.)

Micah: *(Snatches a towel from Jennifer's shoulder.)* Hey! Give me that! It's mine!

Jennifer: Well, sorry. I just found it laying on the floor over there. All I did was pick it up.

Micah: Sure. But next time, why don't you ask first?

Sarah: Micah, you should watch that temper of yours. It's going to get you in trouble one of these days.

Micah: *(Sneering)* Another one of your do's and don'ts, Sarah?

Sarah: Well, the Bible does warn us about anger.

Amy: It does?

Sarah: Yes, it says…

Allison: *(Interrupts.)* We don't want to hear it, Sarah. Really.

Micah: The Bible is so full of do's and don'ts; it's a wonder you Christians have any fun.

Amy: Now, Micah, how can you say that?

Micah: It's really easy, just watch. The Bible is so full of do's and don'ts, it's a wonder you Christians have any fun. See? I said it again. Easier than the first time.

Sarah: But, it's not like that, Micah. We have fun. And besides, losing your temper never does any good, does it?

Micah: It's not against the law, is it?

Sarah: Well, no.

Micah: And it's not even in the Ten Commandments, is it?

Sarah: No, but…

Micah: Then what's the matter with a little temper? My mom says it keeps me from following the crowd, and it makes me strong.

Amy: Sarah and I are strong, and we don't lose our tempers.

Micah: *(Grabs Amy's arm viciously and clenches her teeth.)* I'm tired of this conversation, OK? Drop it! *(Drops Amy's arm.)* Come on, Allison, let's go to English. *(Allison and Micah exit stage right.)*

Sarah: I'm worried about Micah, Amy.

Amy: Me, too, Sarah, but we've done all we can.

Jennifer: Listen, it's no big deal. Lots of people have a temper. *(Picks up her things.)* See you later. *(Exits stage right.)*

Sarah: I just wish they would get it, don't you?

Amy: *(Sighs.)* Yeah, Sarah. Come on, let's get to history class.

(They exit stage right. Micah and Allison enter stage right a few moments later. It is obvious from their actions they have cut class.)

Micah: Let's hide out here, Allison. *(Crosses over to chairs. Sits, opens her purse, and offers Allison a small bag of chips.)*

Allison: Thanks, Micah! *(Takes bag and eats some chips.)* Man, could you believe those two?

(During the following conversation, Allison is to eat most of the bag of chips.)

Micah: You mean Sarah and Amy? *(Reaches for a chip.)*

Allison: Right. They're always griping about one thing or another. It makes me almost glad I'm not a Christian.

Micah: Almost?

Allison: Well, you know. *(Nervously)* I sometimes wonder about God, don't you?

Micah: Do you really? Personally, I haven't given God much thought. The way those two act, you'd think he was just like another teacher or something. Full of rules.

Allison: Some pretty dumb rules, if you ask me.

Micah: (*Laughing*) You said it! (*Reaches for a chip.*) Hey! You ate all of the chips!

(*Micah shoves Allison roughly; Allison almost falls out of her chair.*)

Allison: Hey! Watch it!

Micah: No, *you* watch it! You're a pig.

(*Stands to the sound of a school bell ringing and storms off.*)

Allison: (*Watches Micah in disbelief.*) Maybe there is something to this God stuff after all. (*Slowly picks up things and exits stage right.*)

(*At this point, a minor character walks across the stage with the "Next Day" sign. All enter stage right. Same girls are in the gym.*)

Micah: Gee, Allison, I'm sorry about yesterday. I don't know what came over me.

Allison: (*Grinning*) Should I say hunger?

Amy: What happened yesterday?

Micah: (*Looking at Allison quickly*) Oh, nothing really. Allison and I had a small fight.

Sarah: Your temper again? (*Sighs.*) I wish I could help you with that, Micah.

Allison: (*Quickly*) It was no big deal, Sarah. Just drop it, OK?

Sarah: OK, OK, I will.

(*Ms. Bailey enters stage right.*)

Ms. Bailey: (*Clapping hands*) Girls! Girls! Girls! Are you ready to run track? (*All groan.*) I didn't think so. Why not give me a few laps in here instead?

(*Girls run about three laps, with Ms. Bailey encouraging them.*)

Ms. Bailey: (*Holds up her hand.*) OK, that's enough. You can stop now.

Micah: Thank goodness! I thought I was going to run out of breath there for a moment.

Ms. Bailey: Oh, but you are. I want everyone on the track in ten minutes.

Amy: Ms. Bailey! That's a long way!

Ms. Bailey: (*Grins.*) Yes, it is. So, I suggest you get started, OK? (*Exits stage right.*)

(*All girls bustle with activity.*)

Jennifer: Say, Micah, can I borrow your brush?

Micah: Sure, hang on a second. (*Looks in her bag.*) Wait a minute. It's not here. And my special pen is missing.

Allison: What special pen?

Micah: The one Mike gave me before he left for college. I don't let *anyone* use that pen.

Allison: (*Frowning a bit*) Wait a second, I think I have your brush. You lent it to me in math class this morning, remember?

Micah: (*Suspiciously*) I did? Did I lend you my pen, too?

Allison: (*Hesitantly*) No.

Micah: Let me see. (*Grabs purse from Allison's hand. They struggle. Purse falls to floor, scatters, and pen rolls out. Micah stoops to pick it up.*) You stole my pen! You knew how much it meant to me, and you stole it!

Allison: I did not! I only borrowed it! And you never told me Mike gave it to you. I didn't know!

Micah: *(Shouting)* That's a lie! You're lying! Admit it! *(Begins shoving Allison backward.)*

Sarah: Micah, please don't. You'll hurt her.

Micah: She deserves it! She's a thief! *(Keeps shoving Allison toward the wall.)*

Allison: No, I'm not!

Micah: You are, too!

(Gives Allison one final shove. Allison screams, "hits" head on the mock wall, and falls down.)

Sarah: Oh, no! Allison! *(All rush toward Allison and Micah.)*

Micah: Oh, no! What have I done? Allison! Speak to me!

(Kneels and picks up Allison's head. Allison groans.)

Sarah: I don't think you should move her, Micah. *(She kneels on other side of Allison and begins examining her gingerly.)*

Amy: I'm going to get Ms. Bailey.

Micah: Will she be OK?

◆◆◆ Discussion Activity ◆◆◆

Divide the participants into four groups. Pass out paper and pencils to each group, and have each one select a leader. Say: **The object of this activity is for each group to write an ending to the skit. You will have fifteen minutes.**

Have each group act out the ending they've written. Spend a few moments discussing their choices.

Read Proverbs 14:9 and say: **People ignore some sins because they think they're harmless. Uncontrolled anger is one of those sins that is often ignored.** Ask:

- **What are some others?**
- **Who will suffer more, Allison or Micah? Explain.**
- **How could Sarah and Amy have approached Micah about her sin differently?**
- **Would they have been able to help Micah if they had spoken differently? Why?**
- **What would you have said to Micah about her temper?**

Read Romans 6:23 and ask: **What does death mean in this passage?**

Whose Fault Is It?

Scripture: Matthew 6:25-33

Topic: Suffering

Setting: The scene takes place in the hallway outside a hospital room. Angie and Cassidy are waiting to see Angie's brother, Tim. He and Cassidy have just been in a car accident.

Props: Several chairs should be placed on the stage to resemble a waiting room. If possible, add a small table with a few magazines. Cassidy should have a bandage on her head.

Characters:

Louie—Tim's friend who is a sincere and optimistic person. He knows the Bible and is faithful.

Craig—Tim's pessimistic friend who is confused by the things he sees in the world around him.

Cassidy—Tim's girlfriend who cares for him and believes in him. She is a strong person with a good handle on her faith.

Angie—Tim's sister. She's searching for answers and is distraught by what's happened. She's trying to make sense of the accident.

Nurse—a calm and professional hospital worker

◆◆◆ Script ◆◆◆

(Cassidy and Angie sit together, holding hands. They've been crying. Cassidy has a bandage on her head. Louie and Craig come running in.)

Louie: Cass! Angie! We just heard!

Craig: *(To Cassidy)* Are you OK?

Cassidy: Yeah.

Louie: How's Tim?

(Cassidy and Angie look at each other.)

Angie: It's bad.

Cassidy: *(Trying not to cry)* He's, um, paralyzed. He won't be able to walk.

Craig: No!

Louie: Sure he will. It's just temporary or something, right?

Angie: *(Shakes her head.)* My mom's been in with the doctor.

Craig: *(Sits next to Angie.)* What happened?

Cassidy: *(Stands and paces slowly, trying to piece it together.)* I'm not sure. We were in Tim's car. We were just driving along and talking. It was raining and stuff, you know? The car slid. I just remember seeing this tree coming at us. It hit Tim's side. I remember thinking we were going to hit it. And I remember seeing the dashboard coming closer, like in slow motion, and then…I don't know.

Angie: I know Tim drives too fast sometimes, but…

Cassidy: He wasn't. He was being careful. *(Covers her face.)*

Louie: *(Puts his arm around Cassidy.)* It's OK. Everything's going to be fine.

Angie: *(Stands up.)* No it's not! How can you say that? My brother can't walk! Nothing's ever going to be fine again! *(Walks a few steps away from them with her back turned.)*

Louie: Ang, that's not what I meant…

Cassidy: What did you mean?

Craig: *(Stands.)* He was just trying to be nice. It's not like this is Louie's fault!

Angie: *(Turning back angrily)* Then whose fault is it?

(Everyone stops and looks uncomfortable.)

Craig: *(Sits.)* I don't know.

Angie: *(Stomps toward Cassidy and Louie.)* I know what you're thinking. You're all thinking it's Tim's fault. Well, it's not! He's a good person. God wouldn't do something like this to him!

Cassidy: *(Puts her hand on Angie's arm.)* Nobody thinks that! Right?

Louie: No way.

(There's a pause.)

Cassidy: Craig?

Craig: Well, there's got to be some reason.

Angie: *(Hands on her hips)* Like what?

Craig: *(Looks uncomfortable.)* I don't know. Tim must've done something bad or God wouldn't have made him paralyzed.

Louie: *(Walks away a few paces shaking his head.)* That's what you really think?

Craig: Yeah. Don't you?

Louie: No!

Cassidy: Me neither.

Craig: How else do you explain it?

Angie: It was an accident!

Craig: Yes, I know! But what I'm saying is that there has to be some reason God would punish Tim.

Cassidy: You never actually listen when you go to church, do you?

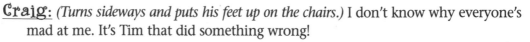

Craig: *(Turns sideways and puts his feet up on the chairs.)* I don't know why everyone's mad at me. It's Tim that did something wrong!

Angie: Stop saying that! *(Walks away a few steps.)*

Louie: *(Sits next to Craig; tries to be patient.)* Look! God doesn't work like that. If we got punished for every little thing we did wrong, we'd all be in trouble all the time.

Cassidy: *(Pushes Craig's feet down and sits next to him.)* Besides, God doesn't do bad things to us.

Craig: *(Challenging)* Yeah, so why do bad things happen? Why do people suffer?

Louie: God gave us the choice if we wanted to do stuff his way or ours. We want to do stuff our way. That's why everything's such a mess.

Craig: *(Stands and takes a few steps, trying to reason the question out.)* But we're Christians, which means we're doing stuff God's way. Tim must've done something that wasn't God's way. That's why God's making him suffer.

Cassidy: Even though we're Christians, we're still human.

Louie: …which means deep down we all really want to do stuff our own way. Being a Christian just means that we realize there's more to it than just us.

Angie: *(Turns to Louie.)* You really think so?

Louie: Don't you?

Angie: Well, I guess I was kind of thinking that what Craig said was true. I mean, I've been trying to think of all the bad things Tim's done and figure out which one was so bad.

Cassidy: That's so unfair to Tim. We're all stupid about a lot of stuff, but God loves us anyway. Isn't that the whole reason Jesus came to earth?

Louie: Yeah, when the Bible says, Jesus died for our sins, it was for all those rotten things we do.

Cassidy: God doesn't just pick and choose which things he forgives us for.

Angie: *(Sits next to Louie.)* I guess that would be sort of weird.

Craig: *(Refuses to give in.)* But some stuff does happen because we sin. I knew this guy who did drugs just once. It was his very first time, and *zap!* God killed him right there.

Louie: God didn't kill him, drugs did.

Craig: What's the difference?

Cassidy: There's a big difference! If you do something that could hurt you, you'll probably get hurt.

Angie: But how do you know if it's God or something else?

Louie: *(Stands up and thinks for a minute.)* OK! If I go stand on a railroad track and get run over by a train, whose fault is it, mine or God's?

Angie: Yours.

Louie: Why?

Angie: Because you were the one who decided to stand there.

Louie: Exactly.

Craig: I get that it would be your fault. But what about some kid on a playground who gets killed when a crazy guy pulls out a gun and shoots everyone? How come God picked that kid to die?

Cassidy: God didn't pick the kid. God didn't have anything to do with it.

Angie: *(Looks at Cassidy.)* It's the crazy guy's fault, right?

Cassidy: Yes!

Angie: *(Quietly, after a pause)* So what about an accident, like Tim's?

Louie: It's just that—an accident! The road was slick.

Angie: *(Hopefully)* So it's not Tim's fault?

Louie: No. Actually, I think God was looking out for him. It could've been a lot worse. They're both still alive.

Cassidy: I was thinking about that.

Craig: *(Still not grasping the idea)* But Tim's never going to walk again. He's going to suffer for this the rest of his life.

Louie: It'll definitely change things. But he doesn't have to see it as suffering. That's another choice.

Craig: That's easy for you to say!

Cassidy: I think Louie's right. Nothing ever gets Tim down. It's not like this will be easy, but maybe we can help him remember what's good in his life.

Craig: Like what?

Angie: He's got friends who care about him. God loves him. That seems like a good start.

(Nurse enters. Angie and Cassidy stand up.)

Nurse: He can see you now, but just for a minute, and only two at a time.

Louie: *(To Angie)* Why don't you and Cassidy go first.

Angie: OK.

(Cassidy and Angie follow the Nurse out.)

Craig: *(Sits down, chin in hand.)* I'm still not sure if I believe all that.

Louie: *(Sits next to him.)* I guess it just comes down to whether you believe that God does things like paralyze people or kill them.

Craig: Yeah, I suppose. *(Pauses.)* I hope Tim's gonna be OK.

Louie: *(Puts his hand on Craig's shoulder.)* Of course he will.

✦✦✦ Discussion Activity ✦✦✦

Discuss the skit using these questions:

● Which character seemed most like you? Give an example of when you have felt the same way as the character.

● Which of the other characters helped you see suffering in a way different than you have before? Explain why.

● If God is good, why does he allow evil things like sickness and death?

● How do you feel about a God who allows suffering?

Say: Consider that Jesus suffered in every way imaginable. People made fun of him. Some accused him of being insane. His friends betrayed him, and he died a terrible and painful death. Ask:

● How does knowing that Jesus suffered in some of the ways we do today, make it easier to pray about our suffering?

● How does knowing that Jesus understands your suffering make you feel?

Read Matthew 6:25-33. Ask:

● Why does Jesus suggest we should have faith rather than worry about the future?

The Test Zone

Scripture: Genesis 39:1-20 and Genesis 41:41-42

Topic: Honesty

Setting: This scene takes place at school.

Props: On one side of the stage, you will need a few desks and chairs arranged in classroom style with a teacher's desk (or table) at the head of the class. Students should have notebooks to carry into the room, and the teacher will need some test papers to hand out. On the other side of the stage, place a podium for the Announcer to use. (Optional props—a tape of *The Twilight Zone* theme to be played whenever the Announcer speaks, and lighting that will alternate from the Announcer to the classroom scene whenever action takes place on either side.)

Characters:

Announcer
Rachel—a Christian teenager
Brooke—Rachel's non-Christian friend
Sean—a teenage boy
Teacher—Mr. or Ms. Johnson
Student #1
A few other students

◆◆◆ Script ◆◆◆

(As the Announcer speaks, the Teacher enters first; then the students enter by twos. Rachel and Brooke enter together. The Teacher goes to the front of the class, while the students stand talking in the back of the classroom.)

(Music swells and recedes whenever Announcer talks.)

Announcer: One of these teenagers is about to enter into a new world—a world of her own making—a world where the choices she makes affects only her. Or do they?

Brooke: Rachel, are you ready for the test today?

Rachel: *(Puzzled)* Test? What test?

Announcer: The door has been opened. She has entered—*the test zone.* How will she handle it?

Sean: Where have you been, girl?

Student #1: Haven't you been going through that book Ms. Johnson assigned us to read?

Rachel: *(Looks about desperately.)* That test is *today?* Oh, no!

Brooke: What's the matter, Rachel?

Rachel: *(Slowly)* I've been so busy with volleyball, schoolwork, and church stuff that I never finished reading the book. And the test is today?

Sean: *(Impatiently)* Yes. Today. Hello, Rachel! Don't you pay attention?

Brooke: Don't worry, Rachel. You will do well.

Rachel: But I shouldn't take the test if I haven't read it. That's not honest.

Brooke: You don't have to tell her you haven't read the book. Just take the test. You can just guess at the answers.

Rachel: But that's not right.

Brooke: Why not?

Announcer: What will Rachel do? What would you do? How would you handle— *the test zone?*

(Rachel, Brooke, and other students sit as Announcer speaks.)

Rachel: *(Worried, speaks to the audience.)* I don't know what I should do!

Sean: *(Hands Rachel a slip of paper.)* Here! I made this for Tony, but he's sick today. *(Grins to show Tony isn't really sick.)*

Rachel: *(Puzzled)* What's this?

Sean: *(Aside to Rachel)* A cheat sheet, of course. If you're careful, Ms. Johnson will never catch you. Honest!

Rachel: *(Echoing)* Catch me? Doing what?

Sean: *(Aside to Brooke)* Where's she from, anyway? *(To Rachel)* Catch you using it to take the test, silly.

Rachel: You mean cheat?

Sean: Now she's getting the picture! *(Shakes head in wonder.)*

Announcer: Rachel's predicament grows worse. If she refuses the cheat sheet, what will Sean say? Her choices are few. What will she do in—*the test zone?*

Rachel: *(Shakes her head and hands the sheet back to Sean.)* Thanks, Sean. I appreciate it. But no, I can't do that!

Sean: *(Shrugs.)* Suit yourself. I tried to help, but you better keep your mouth shut. If Ms. Johnson hears about the cheat sheet, I'll know where she heard it from.

Rachel: I won't say anything, Sean. But I wish you wouldn't use it, really. It will only hurt you in the end. *(Sean shakes his head as they take their seats.)*

Teacher: *(Passing out tests)* No talking, of course. This test covers the first ten chapters of the book. It will count as one-fourth of your six-week grade. And, yes, it is multiple choice.

Sean: *(Glances at Rachel, then raises his hand.)* Ms. Johnson! Ms. Johnson!

Teacher: Yes?

Sean: *(Looking at Rachel)* What if you didn't read the book?

Teacher: Well, you shouldn't take the test. That would be dishonest, wouldn't it? *(Teacher pauses from passing out test papers and looks at Sean. Speaking sternly)* You did read the book, didn't you?

Sean: *(Happily)* Oh, yes, ma'am! I did.

Teacher: Then there shouldn't be a problem. *(Returns to front and sits.)*

Rachel: *(To audience)* Now what? What should I do?

Announcer: Rachel has reached the point of no return. She must choose her course of action and choose it quickly. A course of action that affects only her. Or will it?

Teacher: Do not begin until I give the word.

Rachel: *(Stands abruptly and blurts out.)* Ms. Johnson?

Teacher: Yes, Rachel?

Rachel: *(Sadly)* I can't take the test, Ms. Johnson.

Teacher: Of course you can, Rachel. You'll do fine.

Rachel: No, Ms. Johnson, I can't. *(Shakes her head.)* You see *(pauses)*, I never finished reading the book.

Teacher: *(Stiffens.)* Oh, I see. Well, then bring your paper to me. You realize, of course, this will be a zero.

(Rachel nods morosely as she takes the test to the teacher.)

Teacher: *(Softening)* Thank you, Rachel, for being honest.

(Rachel nods as she hands the test to Teacher and returns to her seat.)

Announcer: Rachel waits quietly while the others take the test. Will her decision have an effect on the others? Why did she choose the path she did? She watches the other students turn in their papers as the class ends, wondering—did she make the right choice?

(All students, except Brooke, take turns getting up, walking to the front of the class, and handing the Teacher their finished tests. Rachel watches each one silently. Teacher motions to Rachel to come to her desk.)

Announcer: But wait. What does the teacher want?

Teacher: Rachel, will you please come up here?

Rachel: *(Stands up as class giggles)* Yes, ma'am.

Teacher: The rest of you are dismissed, if you have finished the test.

(She motions to Rachel, who bends over the table looking at the papers on the Teacher's desk. Rachel nods to Teacher as they "converse." Brooke slowly rises and places her test on Teacher's desk and returns to her seat as other students talk among themselves about the test and leave. Such comments as "Wow, tough test!" or "Man, I'd hate to be in her shoes!" with glances at Rachel and Teacher talking as they exit. Rachel returns to her seat, picks up her books, and starts offstage. She stops as Brooke places a hand on her arm.)

Brooke: *(Stage whisper)* Why did you tell her? No one would have told on you, not even Sean.

Rachel: I know. But I just couldn't take the test. It wouldn't be right.

Brooke: *(In a normal tone)* But she wouldn't have known! And you would have answered some of them right by guessing, even if you didn't use Sean's cheat sheet. At least you would have made better than a zero.

Rachel: Maybe. But I would have known. And, well *(pauses)*, I just couldn't.

Brooke: *(Surprised)* You really mean that, don't you?

Rachel: *(Nods emphatically.)* Oh, yes! And guess what?

Brooke: *(Curious)* What?

Rachel: Ms. Johnson gave me extra credit work to help my grade.

Brooke: *(Astonished)* She did? She never gives anyone any extra credit work! How come?

Rachel: *(Smiling)* Let me explain it to you. *(They walk off.)*

Announcer: Rachel made it through. But, what about you? How will you handle—the test zone?

(Music swells and fades as lights dim and go out.)

◆◆◆ Discussion Activity ◆◆◆

After the skit, ask:
- **If you were Rachel, what would you have done?**
- **What do you think Rachel told Brooke?**
- **What difference would it have made if Rachel had taken the test? Why?**

Say: **In the Bible there are examples of teens who have faced similar situations. One of them was Joseph.**

Briefly tell the story of Joseph's brothers selling him into captivity. Read Genesis 39:1-20. Ask:
- **What do you think happened to Joseph?**

Allow time for responses. Then read Genesis 41:41-42. Ask:
- **What was Rachel's reward for being honest?**
- **Why do you think Rachel and Joseph chose to obey God?**
- **If you were in Rachel's class, what would you have thought of Rachel?**
- **Why do you think Rachel chose to be honest about the test?**
- **What would you do if you were in a similar situation?**
- **How did Rachel's decision affect others, if at all?**
- **Would it have been OK for Rachel to take the test if no one had known? Why or why not?**
- **What makes something dishonest?**

Dark Shadows

Scripture: Matthew 5:38-42

Topic: Violence

Setting: This scene takes place Anywhere, USA.

Props: You'll need two Bibles (one for each narrator), a water gun, a bandanna, and an All-Star or sports jacket for Ted to wear.

Characters:
Narrator #1—narrates the story using Scriptures of love and mercy and wears white. Can be a boy or a girl.
Narrator #2—narrates the story using Scriptures of violence and wears black. Can be a boy or girl.
Ted—main character
Two female characters
Two male characters

◆◆◆ Script ◆◆◆
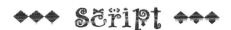

Narrator #1: *(Introduces Ted.)* Good evening, ladies and gentlemen, and welcome to our story. I'd like you to meet Ted who is a rather nice-looking young man.

(Ted enters, waves, flexes his muscles, and strikes a pose with a giant smile.)

Narrator #1: Ted has decided to take a stroll.

(Ted walks around in circles.)

Narrator #1: While on his stroll, Ted will meet many people.

(Ted continues to walk in circles.)

Narrator #2: *(Comes running in.)* Hey, wait a minute, wait for me! I'm in this story too, remember?

Narrator #1: I was trying to forget, actually! *(It is obvious Narrator #1 dislikes Narrator #2.)*

Narrator #2: You haven't started without me have you?

Narrator #1: Well, as a matter of fact…

Ted: *(Still walking in circles.)* Hey, can I stop now? I'm getting a little dizzy!

Narrator #1: Huh? Oh sure. Sorry.

Ted: *(Ted stops and stands there with a grin on his face.)* Thanks!

Narrator #1: No problem! As I was saying, Ted will meet many people, and we will see him react to each one just the way Jesus would.

Narrator #2: Hey look! Here comes somebody!

(They all turn and look.)

Narrator #1: Let's watch...

(A woman enters.)

Ted: Hello, ma'am, how are you?

(She walks up and slaps him on the right cheek.)

Ted: Ouch! Now what did you go and do that for?

Narrator #1: *(Reading from a Bible)* "Do not resist an evil person. If someone strikes you on the right cheek, turn to him the other also" (Matthew 5:39).

Ted: *(Looks at the woman and smiles and then turns his left cheek toward her and points at it.)* OK. Put her right there!

(She slaps him again.)

Ted: Ouch! That hurt! I think she has been practicing! *(He rubs his cheek.)*

Narrator #1: Way to go, Ted! You are on the right track!

Narrator #2: Hey, kid! Listen to this! *(Reads from the Bible.)* "If anyone injures his neighbor, whatever he has done must be done to him: fracture for fracture, eye for eye, tooth for tooth. As he has injured the other, so he is to be injured" (Leviticus 24:19-20). Do you catch my drift, kid?

Ted: *(Looks puzzled for a moment then slaps the lady back.)* How'd you like them apples, missy?

(Woman grabs her cheek and runs off the stage. Narrator #1 puts hands on hips in disgust and looks at Narrator #2 who laughs.)

Man: *(Runs in with a bandanna over his face and a water gun.)* Stick 'em up!

Ted: Huh?

Man: I said, stick 'em up!

Ted: *(To the narrators)* Oh, you have got to be kidding!

Narrator #2: You heard him!

(Ted puts his hands over his head.)

Man: Give me your jacket!

Ted: My jacket? But this is my All-Star jacket!

Man: I said, give me that jacket!

Ted: But I paid a lot of money for this jacket!

Narrator #1: *(Reading again from the Bible)* "If someone wants to sue you and take your tunic, let him have your cloak as well" (Matthew 5:40).

Ted: Hey, let me see that! *(Walks over to the narrator, takes the Bible, reads it for himself. Then he walks over to his previous position, takes off the jacket, and hands it to the man. He also takes off his shirt, leaving a T-shirt on, and hands it to the man.)* Anything else?

Man: Well, I do kind of like those shoes.

Ted: *(Looks down at his shoes and shakes his head for a moment, then takes off his shoes and hands them to the man.)* Here, go, enjoy!

(The man exits.)

Narrator #1: You are doing great so far!

(Ted is rubbing his jaw, where the lady slapped him and wiggling the toes on his bare feet.)

Ted: Thanks!

Narrator #2: *(Shakes head and laughs.)* Kid! Kid! Come over here! Listen to this…"Come now, let's kill him and throw him into one of these cisterns and say that a ferocious animal devoured him" (Genesis 37:19). Look, he took your jacket, he stole your shoes, don't you think you have a right to kill the guy? I mean, who would know? Folks would just think ferocious animals devoured him, you know what I mean?

Ted: *(Looks at Narrator #1 and then back and at Narrator #2 as he scratches his head and looks confused.)* I'm not sure.

Narrator #2: Well of course you are, kid. It's right here in the Good Book, ain't it?

Narrator #1: *(Glares at Narrator #2.)* Give the kid a break, will you?

Narrator #2: Just stick with me kid, you'll be fine.

Narrator #1: *(To Ted)* Don't listen to him, he'll get you in trouble!

Narrator #2: Yeah! Yeah!

Narrator #1: Oh look! Here comes someone else!

Ted: Great!

(A girl enters, not watching where she is going and runs into Ted.)

Ted: Hey! Are you OK?

Girl: You big jerk! You no-good, lowdown, sorry, monkey-looking, squinty-eyed little twerp!

(Ted reacts by feeling his face, his nose, and squinting his eyes as she says these things.)

Ted: Monkey-looking! Squinty-eyed! What?

Narrator #2: I thought you were kind of cute myself!

Ted: Look here, lady…

Narrator #1: *(Reads from the Bible.)* "Love your enemies and pray for those who persecute you" (Matthew 5:44).

Ted: Oh, all right! *(He drops to the ground and prays silently.)*

Narrator #2: "Break the arm of the wicked and evil man; call him to account for his wickedness" (Psalm 10:15).

Ted: Huh? Ohhh! *(He gets up and grabs the girl by the arm and twists.)*

Girl: Ouch! Ouch!

Narrator #1: "Love your neighbor as yourself" (Matthew 22:39).

(Ted stops twisting her arm.)

Narrator #2: "If you will deliver these people into our hands, we will totally destroy their cities" (Numbers 21:2).

(Ted shrugs and picks the girl up.)

Narrator #1: Hold it! Wait a minute! Wait just a cotton-picking minute! Destroy her city? Where did that come from? It makes no sense whatsoever!

Narrator #2: Well, I couldn't think of anything else to say on the spur of the moment.

(Narrator #2 looks at Ted and shrugs shoulders. Ted puts the girl down.)

Girl: *(Walks off.)* Jerk!

Ted: Now that about does it! Did you hear what she said?

Narrator #1: *(Reads from the Bible.)* "Consider it pure joy, my brothers, whenever you face trials of many kinds, because you know that the testing of your faith develops perseverance" (James 1:2-3).

Ted: Joy, huh? *(Laughs comically)* Har…har…har…har…har…I'm so happy!

Narrator #2: I've kind of been enjoying this myself! Well, gotta run. See ya 'round kid!

Ted: Hey, wait a minute! Where are you going?

Narrator #2: I got places to go and people to see!

Ted: But what if I need your help?

Narrator #1: Hey, what am I, chopped liver? You don't need that person.

Ted: But what if I get mad? What if I lose my temper? What should I do?

Narrator #1: *(Reads from the Bible again.)* "My dear brothers, take note of this: Everyone should be quick to listen, slow to speak and slow to become angry" (James 1:19).

Ted: Yes, but…

(Narrator #1 holds the Bible up to read it again with a raised eyebrow.)

Ted: I know, I know, listen to what the Word says!

◆◆◆ Discussion Activity ◆◆◆

Say: **The Bible has a lot to say about violence. But Jesus definitely made it clear that we are to love one another.** Ask:
- How would you react if you were Ted?
- What types of violence are prevalent in our world today?

Say: **Actually, violence started in the days of Adam and Eve, right from the very beginning of human existence when Cain killed Abel.** Ask:
- What are some ways violence might be stopped or controlled today?
- In what ways can we control the way we react toward others?
- What Scriptures surprised you in this skit?

As an end to the discussion, read Matthew 5:38-42.

Help From Above

✦

The Z Tree

Scripture: Luke 19:1-10

Topic: Salvation and Evangelism

Setting: The stage of an auditorium

Props: Three of the characters will need something that looks like pages from a script. One chair should be set in the middle of the stage. You'll also need a tree branch that can be easily held in one hand (either natural or cut from paper).

Characters:
Frank—the youth group sponsor
Amber—a teenage girl
Kit—a teenage boy
Phoenicia—a teenage girl
Stan—a teenage boy

◆◆◆ Script ◆◆◆

Frank: *(Enters from offstage.)* Hello, everybody.

Amber, Kit, Phoenicia, and Stan: Hello, Frank…Hi…How's it going?…*(and so forth.)*

Frank: I'm glad you're all here, and I appreciate your interest in trying out for this year's play. It's called *Zacchaeus Climbs a Tree.*

Amber: We used to sing a song about him in Sunday school.

Kit: I remember.

Amber: How many parts are there in the play?

Frank: Enough for all of you. But the main parts are Jesus and Zacchaeus. These are the parts I want to cast first. Let's see…*(Looks over the young people assessing each for parts.)* Stan, you're pretty average in height. Why don't you read the part of Zacchaeus first?

Phoenicia: Why does his height matter?

Frank: Zacchaeus was a small man. That's why he had to climb a tree to see Jesus. Here, Stan, climb up on this chair. Hold this tree branch near your face, like this. *(Demonstrates before handing the branch to Stan.)* Read the highlighted part of the script.

(Stan stands on the chair holding the branch near his face.)

Kit: Hey, look! It's Stan of the Jungle.

Stan: Very funny.

Frank: No, no, no. It's Zacchaeus. Zacchaeus! We'll all need to learn to say it properly.

Amber, Phoenicia, and Kit: Zacchaeus, Zacchaeus!

Stan: *(Looks a little skeptical.)* Do we have to use that name?

Frank: What do you mean? That name comes straight from the Bible.

Stan: Yeah, but you've got to admit, it lacks a sense of, uh…

Amber: Style?

Phoenicia: Finesse?

Kit: Pizazz?

Stan: I was going to say *pronounce-ability.* It doesn't exactly roll off your tongue. Maybe we could just call him *Mr. Z.*

Phoenicia: Yeah. That sounds good. *Mr. Z.* It has finesse and pro…pro…*(Looks at Stan.)*

Stan: *Pronounce-ability.*

Phoenicia: Thanks! *Pronounce-ability!*

Kit: Is that a real word?

Frank: *Mr. Z Climbs a Tree?* I don't know. It sounds like a nursery rhyme to me.

Phoenicia: You're right. Instead, let's call it *The Z Tree.*

(Frank looks pained.)

Phoenicia: Just think it over, Frank. It has real potential.

Kit: *The Z Tree?*

Frank: OK. We'll see. Stan, are you ready to read the scene where Jesus and Zacchaeus meet?

Stan: Sure. Should I start from the beginning?

Frank: Uh, no. Page three. I'll read the part of Jesus. Phoenicia, you read the narrator's part. *(He hands Phoenicia a script.)* The rest of you listen and see what you think.

(Kit and Amber move to one side.)

Phoenicia: *(Reads from the script.)* Zacchaeus…uh, I mean Mr. Z had trouble finding his way along the road. The crowd was so large that he could not see where he was going. When he came to a large sycamore tree, he climbed up to look around.

Stan: Wow, from here I can just about see the road. Such a crowd! I've never seen so many people—and all for one man.

Phoenicia: Finally the crowd began to stir with excitement. Jesus was coming!

Stan: There he is! I can see him!…Why, he's coming this way!…He's going to pass right under this tree. What luck! I'll get the best view of anyone.

Phoenicia: But Jesus did not pass under the tree. Instead, he stopped and looked right up at the tax collector who stood among the leaves.

Frank: Zacchaeus? Is that you?

Stan: Are you talking to me?

Frank: Yes. Your name is Zacchaeus, isn't it?

Stan: Uh, yes! Yes, it is. *(He adds with a grin.)* But my friends call me Mr. Z.

Frank: *(Frowns.)* Stan. That's not in the script.

Stan: *(Lets the branch fall to his side.)* I know, I just thought I'd try it to see how it sounded. And I'll have to tell you, I like it.

Frank: OK, OK. Let's pick it up from there. *(Returns to the script.)* Hurry out of that tree. I am going to your house today for lunch.

Stan: *You* are going to *my* house. Aren't you afraid of what people will say?

Frank: No, not really. Now hurry.

Stan: Gladly! *(He hops off the chair and puts the branch down.)* Right this way, Jesus.

Phoenicia: And together they headed to Mr. Z's house. But the people in the crowd began to grumble and to mutter to themselves, "Look, Jesus has gone to eat with that sinner."

Frank: OK, Phoenicia. That's far enough. Good job, but I still need to think through this Mr. Z thing.

Amber: Hey, Frank. What's the big deal about being a tax collector?

Frank: What do you mean?

Amber: It sounds like everybody hated Little Z.

Kit: Little Z?

Frank: In those days a tax collector was something different from what we think of. They very often cheated people by charging them too much for their taxes. Actually there were a lot of reasons for people to dislike a tax collector.

Phoenicia: Jesus didn't seem to mind. He was willing to eat lunch with the Z Man.

Kit: The Z Man?

Frank: Exactly! Jesus was willing to talk with Zacchaeus and go to his house. When everyone else thought of Zacchaeus as a rotten person, Jesus came looking for him.

Kit: Jesus came looking for him? Wow!

Frank: Right. Luke's gospel tells us that Jesus "came to seek and to save what was lost." That included Zacchaeus, or Mr. Z, or whoever.

Kit: *(Quietly)* I wish Jesus would come looking for me.

Phoenicia: Me, too.

Frank: What did you say?

Kit: Oh, nothing.

Phoenicia: We were just saying…well, you know…it would be nice to know that someone was looking for you.

Frank: But he is.

Kit: Who is?

Frank: Jesus is. Jesus is looking for all of us. He wants us to know that he loves us and wants us to follow him. When the New Testament says that Jesus called disciples, it means that he invited men and women to serve and obey God. And they weren't all tax collectors either. There were lots of people just like you and me.

Amber: Yeah, but do we have to be in a tree? Or can Jesus find us other places, too?

Frank: Zacchaeus was in a tree, but Jesus looks for us and calls to us wherever we are—at school, at work, or at home with our families. Jesus wants us all to leave behind the wrong things that we do and join him and follow him. Then he promises to give us eternal life. This is what we call salvation.

Amber: So what happened next with the Z Dude?

Kit: The Z Dude! I like that one.

Frank: Well, let's see what the play says. Let's pick it up where we left off. Phoenicia.

Phoenicia: Zacchaeus must have heard the comments of the crowd because soon he turned to Jesus.

Stan: Jesus, I want you to know something.

Frank: Yes, Zacchaeus?

Stan: From this day on, I will never again cheat anyone. I will take only the money that is due, and if I have cheated anyone in the past I will return to them more than I took.

Frank: Good, Zacchaeus. Today you have found salvation.

Phoenicia: And with that they reached Zacchaeus' house.

Frank: OK. That's good. Amber, does that answer your question?

Amber: Yes, it does. The Z Dude gave up all the bad stuff he'd been doing and became a better person because Jesus showed he cared.

Frank: Right. Jesus challenged Zacchaeus to see that his life could be more meaningful, and that in the end neither money nor power is important.

Amber: What *is* important?

Frank: Wow! That is a really good question!

Phoenicia: Knowing that you are loved. That's important. It's enough to know that God loves me, and he challenges me to do what is right with my life.

Frank: If the audience gets that message out of our play, then I think we'll have done a good job. *(He pauses.)* Now about the name. Don't you think that *Z Dude* is just a little weird?

Amber, Kit, Phoenicia, and Stan: No, it's great…gotta lighten up…get with the times *(and so forth)*.

Frank: We'll see.

◆◆◆ Discussion Activity ◆◆◆

Have the group discuss the skit by asking:
- **What are the most common activities and events in your daily life?**
- **What do they say about you as a person?**

- What kind of person was Zacchaeus before he met Jesus?
- How did Zacchaeus change after meeting Jesus?
- What does the story of Zacchaeus tell you about salvation?
- How is Zacchaeus like you? How is he different?
- In what ways might you change your life in response to Jesus' call to you?

If only God Would Be More Obvious

Scripture: Matthew 28:20

Topic: God's Presence

Setting: Ashley is at home, trying to find God's presence in her life.

Props: On one side of the stage is a small table with a telephone. There are a couple of chairs in the middle. On the other side there is a door, which can be real or imaginary. God's Presence needs a sign that reads **"I AM HERE."**

Characters:

Ashley—a girl who is looking for God's presence in her life, but isn't paying attention to all the ways he shows it

God's Presence—a person holding a sign that says "I AM HERE" (the sign should always face the audience). The characters never see the person portraying God's Presence, even though God's Presence uses big, expressive and comic gestures.

Ringer—a person who makes phone and doorbell-ringing noises. (You might also consider using a tape recorder for the ringing sounds.)

Teresa—Ashley's friend, who understands God is with her, even when things are difficult

◆◆◆ Script ◆◆◆

Ashley: *(To the audience)* You know, something is really bugging me. Last Sunday our minister was talking about finding God's presence in our lives. Wouldn't that be something if God really was present all the time?

God's Presence: *(Comes in and circles Ashley, holds the sign above her head, and moves it all around her—but not in front of her face.)*

Ashley: But I just can't see it.

God's Presence: *(Sighs a big sigh.)*

Ashley: And I really have been looking.

God's Presence: *(Taps foot and shakes head.)*

Ashley: Like the other day…(*Moves to another part of the stage and kneels next to a phone on a small table. God's Presence follows her.*) I was praying about this guy I'm dating. I kind of had this feeling that he's not as great as I thought. It seems like he pays lots of attention to other girls. So I was praying that God would help me make a good decision about what to do. I prayed and prayed, but I never heard from God. Luckily, though, my friend, Marcy, called. (*Phone rings. Ashley stands and picks it up.*)

God's Presence: (*Moves all around her again, waving sign.*)

Ashley: Hello? (*Pause.*) Oh, hi, Marcy! (*Pause.*) Yeah, I was just praying about him. (*Pause.*) You saw him kissing who? (*Pause.*) That's it. He's history! (*Slams the phone down.*) Good thing Marcy was at the movies last night!

God's Presence: (*Drops arms to sides and shakes head again.*)

Ashley: Anyway, as I was saying, I'm just not sure that God really is present all the time.

(*Doorbell rings. Ashley goes to the other side of the stage. Teresa is at the door.*)

God's Presence: (*Follows Ashley and moves all around Teresa.*)

Teresa: (*Sadly*) Hi.

Ashley: What's wrong? You look really upset. (*To audience*) This is my best friend in the world. She's usually much happier than this. (*Leads Teresa to the middle of the stage to sit down.*)

Teresa: My dad's really sick. He's in the hospital.

God's Presence: (*Puts arm around Teresa.*)

Ashley: That's terrible! Are you OK?

Teresa: I think so. I was feeling kind of down, so my mom said I could stop by here before I went back to see him.

Ashley: That's good. You know, lately I've been wishing that God would show himself to me more. Now would be a great time, wouldn't it?

God's Presence: (*Holds sign over Teresa's head and points to it.*)

Teresa: But he is here.

God's Presence: (*Nods vigorously.*)

Ashley: (*Skeptical*) How can you tell?

God's Presence: (*Hands the sign to Teresa.*)

Teresa: I can just feel it. I was so scared and upset when I found out about my dad. Then I started praying, and pretty soon I felt better—you know, more peaceful.

Ashley: How do you know it was God?

God's Presence: (*Shakes head, and with a big, silent sigh, puts head in hands.*)

Teresa: Faith, I guess. What else could it be? Wasn't that the whole reason I was praying?

God's Presence: (*Smiles broadly and pats Teresa on the head.*)

Teresa: Listen, I've got to go. My mom's waiting. I just wanted to tell you what was going on. (*Stands up.*)

God's Presence: *(Takes sign back as she stands up.)*

Ashley: I wish there was something I could do to help.

Teresa: *(Hugs Ashley.)* Just listening helps. You're another way I know God's with me.

God's Presence: *(Kneels down in front of Ashley and Teresa and points from sign to Ashley and back again several times.)*

Ashley: Call me, OK?

Teresa: I will. Thanks. *(Exits.)*

Ashley: *(To audience)* I wish I could have that kind of faith.

God's Presence: *(Falls over in exasperation.)*

Ashley: In any case, things are going pretty well in my life, even if I can't see God's presence. I'm doing OK in school. I have great friends and my family loves me—even if they do drive me crazy sometimes. Yeah, all in all, life isn't so bad.

God's Presence: *(Stands up and hits Ashley on the head with the sign, then holds it up in front of her face, lowers it, and waits expectantly.)*

Ashley: *(Surprised)* I just had a thought! Maybe all these good things in my life are because of God.

God's Presence: *(Skips slowly around Ashley and moves back and forth behind her with the sign overhead.)*

Ashley: *(Getting excited about the idea)* Maybe God is with me all the time, and I just haven't realized it! Wow, can you imagine?

Ashley: *(Slowly looking skeptical)* I don't know. It's just so hard to tell.

God's Presence: *(Slowly stops skipping as Ashley talks.)*

Ashley: I just wish God would do something really obvious so I'd know for sure. Well, I'm off to youth group. We just got this great new youth pastor! *(Exits.)*

God's Presence: *(Leans over with hands on knees, watches Ashley exit, shrugs at audience, and runs off after her.)*

◆◆◆ Discussion Activity ◆◆◆

Lead a short discussion using the following questions:

● **What are some of the ways to know God is present even if we don't always feel he's there?**

● **How is faith important during the times we don't feel God?**

● **Describe a time when you didn't feel God's presence, but later you realized he was actually present in your life.**

● **What can we do to remind ourselves to seek God's presence every day?**

Whatever Floats Your Boat: An Allegory of Grace

Scripture: Ephesians 2:8-9

Topic: Grace

Setting: This scene takes place on "The River of Life," an imaginary river.

Props: Seeker is in a rubber inner tube with a notepad and pencil. Works is on a makeshift raft with a pile of blocks. Grace is in a boat with a paddle, an umbrella, and a fishing pole. (The raft and boat can be made of cardboard or other materials.) Grace and Works are each wearing a sign with their respective names printed large enough so that the audience can easily see them (use construction paper with string to hang signs around the actors' necks).

Characters:

Seeker—a person who doesn't know what grace is and is looking for the answer

Works—a person who thinks good works get you to heaven. Works constantly stacks the blocks and knocks them down again, sometimes one or two, sometimes most of them.

Grace—a person who is aware of God's grace

◆◆◆ Script ◆◆◆

(Works and Grace are onstage in their respective boats. Works is carefully stacking blocks. Grace is enjoying the sun.)

Seeker: *(Jumps into the river in the inner tube.)* Hello!

Works: *(Waving to Seeker but not looking up, he knocks one of his blocks off.)* Oops! Oh, hi!

Grace: Hi. How are you?

Seeker: I'm not sure. I'm seeking something.

Grace: Let me know if I can help.

Seeker: Will do. *(Paddles toward Works.)* What are you doing?

Works: I'm working on my relationship with God.

Seeker: Great! That's exactly what I'm looking for. What's with the blocks?

Works: I'm trying to get closer to heaven.

Seeker: I don't get it. How are you going to get closer to heaven by stacking up blocks and knocking them down?

Works: *(A little embarrassed)* Well, it's actually just the *stacking up* part that's getting me closer.

Seeker: So what's with knocking some of them down? *(Thinks for a moment, then realizes the answer.)* Oh! So I guess you lose ground when they fall. That's gotta make for a stressed out life! *(Watches for another moment.)* How long do you think this is going to take you? I mean, assuming that you're mostly stacking them up?

Works: Well, I'm trying to be good. *(Puts one block on the stack.)* I try to follow the Ten Commandments. *(Adds another block.)* I try to love my neighbor as myself. *(Adds one more block.)*

Seeker: *(Writes down what Works is saying.)* You should get there pretty quick at that rate.

Works: *(Proudly)* Yeah! I'm doing good, aren't I? *(Knocks three blocks off.)* But I do have this little problem with pride.

Seeker: So I see. *(Laughs and makes a note.)*

Works: Don't laugh at me, you jerk! *(Knocks down another block.)* See what you made me do? *(Knocks down another block.)*

Seeker: It looks as if you have a problem with pride and with your temper.

Works: *(Takes a deep breath.)* That was an unkind remark, but I forgive you. *(Adds a block to the stack.)* I will try to learn from your rudeness and be nice to people who are having problems. *(Adds another block.)*

Seeker: So you really think this is going to get you to heaven?

Works: Of course it will. We have to be good to get to heaven. We have to build a foundation of good works to climb up.

Seeker: What if something unexpected happens?

Works: Like what?

Seeker: *(Points downstream.)* Like those rapids we're about to hit.

(All three characters pretend to go through bumpy rapids. Works accidentally knocks most of the blocks down.)

Works: Argh! Why didn't you warn me, you stupid Seeker? *(Knocks down another block.)* This is all your fault! *(Knocks down another block.)* I will get calm. I will be nice. *(Adds a block.)* I will forgive this person. *(Adds another block.)* Even though it's not my fault and that dumb Seeker should have told me those rapids were coming! *(Knocks down two blocks, looks at how few blocks are stacked, and screams in frustration.)*

Grace: It's sad, isn't it?

Seeker: What?

(Seeker paddles with hands over to Grace, while Works continues to stack blocks and knock them down.)

Grace: *(Gestures all around.)* Missing everything that God's given you because you're so wrapped up in keeping score. I've tried to explain it, but it's no use.

Seeker: Explain it to me. What's God given you?

Grace: Everything! I get to be in heaven with him because he loves me so much. *(Puts up umbrella.)*

Seeker: How'd you manage that?

Grace: I didn't. God's Son, Jesus, came to earth as a real person. He died in my place. It was as though he got the punishment for all the bad things I was ever going to do.

Seeker: Just you?

Grace: No, for everyone!

Seeker: Not for me. I never even knew the guy. Why would he be punished for me?

Grace: I told you, because he loves you.

Seeker: So you're saying that you're just going to float along like that and get to heaven?

Grace: No. I'm going to try to do all the things God wants me to, and I'm going to pray for his help to do them. *(Starts to fish.)*

Seeker: Yeah, but what if you don't do what God wants?

Grace: Then I apologize.

Seeker: Does it work?

Grace: Yes! Every time.

Seeker: You don't have to go back upriver or get out and swim for awhile?

Grace: No.

Seeker: And you'll get to go to heaven?

Grace: Absolutely! Isn't that amazing?

Seeker: *(Takes notes.)* It's great! You can do anything you want and nothing happens to you! What a deal!

Grace: It's not like that.

Seeker: But you just said…*(Flips back the notebook pages to find what Grace said.)*

Grace: I said I'm going to try to do what God wants me to.

Seeker: But lightning doesn't strike you if you mess up?

Grace: Right. God's love, understanding, and forgiveness are always there.

Seeker: That's my point!

Grace: No, the point is that what Jesus did for us is so wonderful that we want to do what God wants. It's a way of saying thanks.

Seeker: *(Sees more rapids coming up and smiles.)* So you just let whatever happens happen and chalk it up to what God wants?

Grace: *(Seeing rapids, pulls out paddle.)* We have to take some responsibility.

(All three characters pretend to go through bumpy rapids. Works knocks most of the blocks down again. Grace paddles.)

Grace: I'm not a puppet that God controls.

Seeker: So let me get this straight. *(Consults notebook.)* You live your life as it goes, trying to find out what God wants you to do, and then you do it.

Grace: Yep!

Seeker: When you don't do what God wants, you just say "sorry" and all is forgiven?

Grace: Well, you have to mean it.

Seeker: Aha! *(Points at Grace.)* I knew there was a catch!

Grace: What would be the point of saying you're sorry if you don't mean it? That would be living a lie.

Seeker: OK, I see your point. So then everything you do, you try to do it for God as a way of saying thank you.

Grace: Exactly.

Seeker: And if you don't, God still loves you?

Grace: You've got it.

Seeker: And that's how you get to heaven? That really seems too good to be true.

Grace: It does, doesn't it? *(Relaxes back under the umbrella.)*

Seeker: *(Scratches head and paddles over to Works.)* How's it coming?

Works: Don't even ask. Those last rapids really did me in. I'm going to have to go to church three times a week just to catch up! Good thing they added those midweek services! *(Stacks two more blocks.)*

Seeker: I guess so. Do you really think you'll be able to keep this up your whole life?

Works: I don't have a choice! When I die, God's going to look at everything I've done and want to know why I deserve to be in heaven.

Seeker: Grace over there said we don't have to do anything. God's Son, Jesus, did it for us.

Works: Well, yeah, I know that. But I have to prove I'm worthy.

Seeker: How do you know when you've stacked enough blocks?

Works: I don't! That's why I can't ever stop! What if I worked my whole life and am just a few blocks short in the end?

Seeker: But what if God loved you enough that it wouldn't matter?

Works: *(Stops for a moment.)* That would be great, wouldn't it? *(Goes back to the blocks.)* It's been fun chatting with you, but I've really got to concentrate here.

Seeker: *(Watches Works for a moment. Looks at Grace, who is fishing.)* I guess it comes down to whether you believe that God loves you enough. It doesn't make sense that Jesus would die for only part of the stuff we do wrong. How would you figure out which part? *(Paddles over to Grace.)*

Grace: How's your seeking going?

Seeker: I think I'm done seeking.

Grace: So you found your answer?

Seeker: Yeah! I think God wants us to realize that he loves us no matter what, and he just wants us to love him back.

Grace: Exactly. Hey, you want to fish for awhile?

Seeker: Sure! *(Takes fishing rod.)* What a beautiful day!

◆◆◆ Discussion Activity ◆◆◆

Tape a large piece of newsprint on the wall that says "It Takes 50 Points to Get to Heaven." Write out each of the listed activities separately on different cards. Prepare enough so that each person in your group will receive five cards. Make any number of each category, except Grace; make only two or three "Grace" cards.

Activities

- Going to church: +10 points
- Saying your prayers: +10 points
- Reading the Bible: +10 points
- Telling the truth: +10 points
- Being nice to someone: +5 points
- Not spreading gossip: +5 points
- Asking for forgiveness: +5 points
- Being polite: +5 points
- Skipping church: 10 points
- Being mean: -10 points
- Thinking bad thoughts: -10 points
- Lying: -5 points
- Cheating: -5 points
- Disobeying your parents: -5 points
- Grace

Place the cards in a box or basket, and have each participant choose five. Ask for a volunteer to be the scorekeeper. Have the participants take turns giving their names and reading their cards. The scorekeeper should write their names on the paper and add up each participant's score. Instruct the scorekeeper to draw a halo over the name of any person who receives fifty or more points. If a participant has a "Grace" card, the scorekeeper is to cross off all the person's points and draw a halo over his or her name. When everyone has finished, give the participants who achieved at least fifty points, or a "Grace" card, a small prize such as a candy bar. (**Note:** It is not possible to achieve fifty points in this game.)

After the game, ask:

- **Why do people think they have to earn their way to heaven by doing good works?**
- **If you have received God's grace, why does it not matter how many good works you do?**
- **In what ways do you receive God's grace in your life?**

After the discussion, be sure to give the same small prize to everyone else in the group.

Will the Real Christian Please Step Up!

Scripture: John 3:16

Topic: Salvation

Setting: The scene opens with one character who has the flu lying on a sofa in an apartment.

Props: You'll need some furniture to make the room look like a living room, a thermometer, and a box of tissues. Also include lots of Bibles, Christian T-shirts, jewelry, caps, buttons, stickers, and a sack to hold all the items. You'll also need a CD player and a CD of contemporary Christian music.

Characters:
Jana—a Christian and Teri's roommate, who has the flu
Teri—a first-day Christian with preconceived notions about Christianity

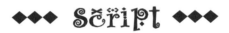 Script

Jana: *(Sneezes, coughs, blows her nose, and takes her temperature as the door opens. She talks with the thermometer in her mouth.)* There you are! Where have you been?

Teri: It's Sunday, where do you think I've been? *(She has a happy tone in her voice and waltzes around humming the tune to a Christian worship song, jazzing it up a little and snapping her fingers.)*

Jana: I don't know, I give up. A jazz festival?

Teri: No, silly! Guess again.

Jana: Teri *(sneezes and coughs)*, I really don't feel like guessing right now!

Teri: Oh, go ahead, it will make you feel better!

Jana: Teri, really I…

Teri: Oh, come on, I'll bet you will never be able to guess.

Jana: *(Sneezes.)* I don't know, the health club?

Teri: Do I usually go to the health club on Sunday mornings?

Jana: No, you usually sleep in on Sunday mornings while I go to church. But no, not today—not the first day I have stayed home in I don't know when *(sneezes and coughs)*—today when I could have used your help as I lie here dying…

Teri: *(Laughs.)* OK, OK, I get the point. Can I get anything for you?

Jana: Just another box of ti…ti…tis…sues! *(Sneezes.)*

Teri: *(Hands Jana a box of tissues from a table.)* I did it, Jana, I finally did it!

Jana: Did what?

Teri: Listened to what you've been telling me all these years. I went to church this morning, and I got myself saved!

Jana: *(Falls off the couch coughing and sneezing.)* You did what?

Teri: I got saved! I went down this morning, and I got saved! I'm a Christian! *(She sings this line to the tune of a worship song.)* I am part of the family of God…

Jana: *(Jumps up and hugs Teri.)* That's great, Teri. I am so happy for you! I wish I could have been there.

Teri: Me too! But I was afraid if I waited, I might chicken out or something!

Jana: Well, congratulations!

Teri: Thank you. What do I do now?

Jana: What do you mean?

Teri: Well, I don't know what I'm supposed to do now. You've been a Christian for a long time. I thought maybe you could tell me what comes next.

Jana: I see. Well, you need to grow in your relationship with God.

Teri: How do I do that?

Jana: Set aside some time every day to spend with God. You can pray, read Scripture…Do you have a Bible?

Teri: No, I don't have any religious…stuff.

Jana: Well, the first thing you need is a Bible.

Teri: OK, well, that's what I will do! *(Puts on her coat.)*

Jana: Where are you going?

Teri: To get myself a Bible. Can I get you anything while I'm out?

Jana: *(Sneezes, coughs, and blows her nose.)* Yeah, a miracle cure for the flu.

(Teri exits for a moment, and Jana leaves the room. After a moment, Teri returns carrying an armload of Bibles, books, and sacks full of Christian items.)

Teri: Jana! Jana! Come and look at all the cool stuff I found! *(She starts taking things out of the sack: T-shirts, keychains, bookmarks, and so forth.)* Jana!

Jana: *(Sneezes and coughs.)* I'm coming, I'm coming.

Teri: Look at all this cool Christian stuff. Now everybody will know that I'm a Christian!

Jana: That's nice.

(Jana turns around to return to her room, and Teri grabs her arm and pulls her back to the sofa where she has dumped all the stuff.)

Teri: Look! Have you ever seen so many cool things before?

Jana: *(Picks through the pile of Bibles.)* Why did you buy so many Bibles? All you need is one!

Teri: Well, I didn't know which one to get, so I got one of each. You didn't tell me they made so many different kinds. Just look at this: King James, New Revised King James, NIV, American Standard, Study Bible, Devotional Bible, Holy Bible, The Message...I just didn't know which one was the real thing.

Jana: They are all the real thing, silly, just different versions!

Teri: Oh...well which one should I use?

Jana: Try this one. It's the one I use. *(She picks up one and hands it to Teri.)*

Teri: Great, thanks.

Jana: *(Sneezes and coughs.)* I think I will go back to bed now if you don't mind.

Teri: Oh, no, I don't mind at all. I will just stay in here and read the Bible.

Jana: Good night. *(Jana exits.)*

Teri: Good night. *(Teri stretches out her arms and looks at the Bible.)* OK...(pats it nervously) all right...just you and me...(She sets it down on the table and walks around it a couple of times, staring at it anxiously. Finally, she sits down and just looks at it.) Well...here we are...(She taps her fingers on the table, looks around the room and then back at the Bible, nervously, chewing her nails.) Excuse me! (She jumps up and runs over to the door that Jana exited through and knocks.) Oh, Jana...Jana!

Jana: *(Yells from offstage.)* What?

Teri: I, uh...I don't exactly know where to start!

Jana: *(Continues to talk from offstage.)* Start what?

Teri: Reading the Bible. I don't know where to start.

Jana: *(Offstage)* Just start with what interests you!

Teri: Right! OK! Thanks! Sorry to bother you. *(She walks back over to the Bible and slowly picks it up, starts to thumb through it, then closes her eyes, stops, and points to a passage.)* OK, here goes...1 Chronicles 2...42..."The sons of Caleb the brother of Jerahmeel: Mesha his firstborn, who was the father of Ziph, and his son Mareshah, who was the father of Hebron. *(Has trouble pronouncing the names.)* The sons of Hebron: Korah, Tappuah, Rekem and Shema." Hmmm. "Shema was the father of Raham, and Raham the father of Jorkeam. Rekem was the father of Shammai." Are these people or whales at Sea World? "The son of Shammai was Maon, and Maon was the father of Beth Zur." Well, of course! Who else? I must be missing something here. Didn't these people ever have any girls? Maybe I should try reading something else. *(She turns back in the Bible.)* Maybe I am just getting ahead of myself...OK, here we go, Exodus 38:9..."Next they made the courtyard..." all right, something I can understand! OK, "next they made the courtyard. The south side was a hundred cubits long and had curtains of finely twisted linen, with twenty posts and twenty bronze bases, and with silver hooks and bands on the posts. The north side was also a hundred cubits long and had twenty posts and twenty bronze bases, with silver hooks and bands on the posts." *(She closes the Bible.)* Is this a Bible or a geometry book? I don't know, maybe I'm just a little dense or something, but I don't get it. OK, OK, I'll just do something different…Let's see, first of all, I need to change my image. I'll start with saying things like uhhh…oh I know! I'll say things like "Hallelujah" or "Amen!" What else do church people say? Oh yeah, they say "bless-ed" a lot, and…umm…oh, they say "I'll pray for you." So when I go to work tomorrow, I will just walk in and say, "Good morning! What a bless-ed day! Hallelujah! Praise the Lord! Amen! I'll be praying for all you sinners!" Hey, that's pretty good. "Hallelujah!" *(Laughs to herself.)* OK, next, I need to look like a Christian; no more designer clothes for me. From now on I am going to wear only Christian T-shirts and Christian jewelry and Christian hats, and Christian every-thing! *(She begins putting on the Christian articles that she talks about until she looks like a walking billboard.)* All right, that's better, now everybody will know that I'm a Christian! Next, I'll plug in this new CD.

(Any contemporary Christian music can be used here. The music is so loud that Jana enters.)

Jana: *(Yells.)* What is going on? What are you doing? *(She walks over and turns off the music.)* What are you doing?

Teri: I'm practicing being a Christian!

Jana: Practicing being a Christian?

Teri: Yeah, I figured, you know, I need to look like I have a little experience in case someone should ask me a question or something. Besides, I tried reading the Bible like you told me. But I didn't understand what it was talking about. So if I want to get into heaven, I figured I better start practicing on at least looking like a Christian and talking like one. Listen to this: "Good morning! What a bless-ed day! Hallelujah! Amen! I'll be praying for you sinners! Hallelujah!" How does that sound?

Jana: Fine if you're preaching a revival! *(Sneezes.)*

Teri: What do you mean by that?

Jana: Teri, when you spoke with the minister this morning, did you believe in your heart that Jesus is the Son of God and that he died for your sins?

Teri: Yes.

Jana: And you know that nobody is perfect, right?—that we have all sinned?—that God loves us no matter what we've done, and his Son, Jesus, died in our place so that we can be forgiven? You understand that, right?

Teri: Yes, I think so.

Jana: So you see, Teri, this morning when you said that you accepted Jesus into your heart and life, God accepted you, knowing that you didn't understand everything in the Bible. He doesn't care! And God doesn't care if you look a certain way or talk a certain way. God just wants you to spend time with him and let him teach you the things that you don't know. It's not what you wear or what you know or how many *churchy* words that you can think of that make you a Christian. It's your faith in God!

Teri: Really?

Jana: Definitely!

Teri: But what if I never understand the Bible?

Jana: You will! In time, you will. There are two Scriptures that I want to share with you right now that I know you can understand. *(She picks up the Bible and turns to Jeremiah 33:3.)* "Call to me and I will answer you and tell you great and unsearchable things you do not know." Teri, pray and ask God to help you understand his Word, and he will.

Teri: Jana, I don't even know how to pray!

Jana: It's easy, you just talk to God like you're talking to me. Tell God how you feel, and ask him to help you.

Teri: But I…it's…I…I've never prayed before…I don't know any…

Jana: You don't have to know one. It's not like a poem. You just talk to God…just be yourself. God is always there and willing to listen, because he loves us. God loves you and me and all of us so much "that he gave his one and only Son…

Jana and Teri: …"that whoever believes in him shall not perish but have eternal life." *(They smile at each other, and then Teri sneezes, as they both laugh.)*

◆◆◆ Discussion Activity ◆◆◆

After the skit, have two people come up. One should be dressed in a Christian T-shirt, wearing Christian jewelry and so forth. The other person should be wearing either clothing that is dirty and ragged, or simply normal clothes. Ask group members if they can spot which one is the Christian. Have the person dressed in Christian attire improvise a bad attitude and gossip to the other person about someone. Instruct the other person to give a Christian response.

Ask:

● **How do you know whether someone is a real Christian?**

● **Why are we unable to identify a Christian by the clothes he or she wears?**

● **If someone appears to be nice, does that mean he or she is a Christian? Explain your answer.**

● **What does it mean to be a Christian?**

Truth or Dare

Scripture: John 8:32 and Philippians 2:9-11

Topic: Salvation and Truth

Setting: The set serves first as a living room and later as heaven.

Props: You will need two chairs and a newspaper at stage right and a small table with a telephone at stage left. The small table will also serve as a place for the Angel to stand behind during the heaven scene at the end of the skit. The angel will carry a book.

Characters:

Beth—a non-Christian teenage girl seeking the truth in all the wrong places

Jill—a Christian teenage girl who knows the absolute truth about God and tries unsuccessfully to share it with her best friend, Beth

Angel—a girl or boy dressed in white

◆◆◆ Script ◆◆◆

(The scene opens with Beth and Jill standing at center stage with their backs to the audience. Beth walks over and sits down in a chair on one side of the stage and starts reading a newspaper.)

Jill: *(Walks over to Beth and sits down in a chair next to her.)* Hi, Beth.

Beth: *(Keeps her head in the newspaper.)* Hi.

Jill: Whatcha doing?

Beth: I'm reading my horoscope.

Jill: Your horoscope? May I see that?

(Beth hands Jill the newspaper, and Jill begins reading it.)

Jill: "While Mercury insists there is no need to worry about the past, Venus will bring you great understanding of the traumas of the past weeks and the zodiac will re-solve questions about a dramatic hidden advantage that is moving your way." *(To Beth)* This is crazy! What is this stuff?! Do you really believe this?

Beth: Oh, I don't know. It's kind of fun to read it and see if any of it comes true.

Jill: Beth, there is no truth in any of this! It's just a bunch of hogwash!

Beth: Is there any truth, Jill, really? I mean, how can we be sure of anything?

Jill: I guarantee you there is no truth in any of this stuff! Trust me! If you want to know the truth, you can borrow my Bible.

Beth: We've been through this before, Jill. You know that I don't believe in anything that I can't see.

Jill: I wish you knew what I know…I wish I could take your heart into my heart and show you how it feels to know the real truth.

Beth: But you can't, so let's just drop it.

(They both walk back over to center stage and turn their backs toward the audience for a brief pause. After a moment, Beth walks over to the other side of the stage, picks up the phone, and starts dialing.)

Jill: *(After a moment, Jill walks over to Beth.)* Hey, Beth, you want to go to the mall with me?

Beth: Shhh. I'm on the phone.

Jill: Sorry.

Beth: *(Responds to the conversation on the other end of the phone.)* Wow! That's great! I can't believe this…how many children will I have?

Jill: *(Raises an eyebrow.)* Who are you talking to?

Beth: The Psychic Answer Network. They said that I will be…

Jill: *(Jerks the phone from her hand and hangs it up.)* Give me that phone! Are you crazy?

(She places the phone under the table.)

Beth: Why did you go and do that?

Jill: In the first place, those people charge you about a trillion dollars a minute. In the second place, they don't know what they're talking about!

Beth: How do you know?

Jill: Just trust me on this, OK? We've been best friends for a long time. I wouldn't lie to you!

(Beth shrugs and follows Jill. They both walk back to center stage with their backs facing the audience. After a brief pause, Beth turns around and goes to sit in the middle of the floor. She faces the audience with her legs crossed Indian-style and hums loudly.)

Beth: Ahhhh…uhmmm…Ahh…uhmmm.

(In a moment Jill turns around and walks over to her.)

Jill: Beth, what are you doing?

(Beth ignores her.)

Jill: Beth…Beth!

Beth: *(Continues to hum as she answers Jill.)* What? Ahhh…uhmmm…Ahhh…uh-mmm…

Jill: What are you doing?

Beth: *(She speaks the same way she hums.)* I'm meditating…uhmmm…Ahhh…uh-mmm…

Jill: Oh! *(Pause.)* Why?

Beth: *(Again she speaks in this humming style, never missing a beat.)* I learned it from my new boyfriend…Ahhh…uhmmm…

Jill: Oh, for crying out loud, will you please stop that! *(Grabs her arm and pulls her up.)* What new boyfriend?

Beth: Moonbeam.

Jill: Moonbeam?

Beth: That's right! Moonbeam!

Jill: And just where did you meet this Moonbeam?

Beth: You mean in this life or my last one?

Jill: Excuse me?

Beth: Well you see, Moonbeam said that we met in a past life, except that he was a tree and I was the grass that grew around his trunk. That's why we have such a strong bond, because we spent so much time growing close to each other.

Jill: Oh brother!

Beth: We met this time at the laundromat. My red sock was stuck to his white shirt in the dryer. It was incredible! The karma between us is unmistakable!

Jill: And just what was your sock doing in the dryer with his shirt?

Beth: I left it in there by mistake. Only now I know it wasn't a mistake; it was karma. It was one of those mystical moments, you know! Full of superkinetic power!

Jill: This is getting better all the time!

Beth: So after we separated my sock from his shirt, he took me to the Fellowship of Oneness.

Jill: Fellowship of Oneness?

Beth: Oh Jill, you really must join us one evening. It is so spiritual. Moonbeam taught me that we are one within ourselves, and that we are to worship within the temple of our being through meditation.

Jill: Wait a minute. Moonbeam told you to...you're kidding me, right?

Beth: Now, Jill, don't be such a skeptic!

Jill: That is about the most absurd thing I have ever heard of! There is only one God and his name *ain't* Moonbeam!

Beth: That's not funny, Jill!

Jill: Who's being funny? I'm telling you, that is ridiculous!

Beth: I really don't appreciate you saying that. You don't see me going around making fun of you!

Jill: That's because I don't go around making friends with past-life gurus named Moonbeam! I mean...what kind of name is that? Moonbeam!

Beth: I think it is a lovely name!

Jill: Are you blind? This guy is really twisted! We don't have a past life, none of us! We only get one go at it. Do you hear me? *One—numero uno!* That's it! That's all! You can't worship *(mockingly)* "the oneness in the temple of your being." It just doesn't work that way! How can you even dare to believe all that! Look, Beth, you've gotta trust me on this. I'm your best friend. I wouldn't lie to you! That stuff is just a bunch of hoopla that somebody made up.

Beth: *(Looks confused and hurt.)* Yeah…well, how do you know that everything in your Bible isn't made up? At least I can see what I'm dealing with here. I know myself and what I'm capable of. I understand the oneness of my being! Maybe you should give it a try!

Jill: Beth, will you stop with the "oneness of my being" stuff? It doesn't exist! Not at all, none, *nada*, zip! There is nothing to that! But God…God is as real as the air that you breathe. You can't see it, but you know it's there. And when the wind blows, you can see how it moves even the hair on your head. You can see the things it affects, right?

Beth: Yes, I guess so.

Jill: It's the same with God. Even though you can't see God, he is there! You can see the effect God has on people's lives, just like when the wind blows. Look around; you can see God. He is real! That is the truth!

Beth: I don't know, Jill. I just don't know what to think anymore. *(Pauses.)*

Jill: Come on, let's just forget it. We'll go out and get ourselves a supersonic banana split and check out the karma between the toppings, OK?

Beth: Ha…ha!

Jill: Oh, come on! That'll take our minds off it.

(They both laugh.)

Beth: Sure, why not!

(They get up and walk back to center stage with their backs to the audience. After a brief pause, they both turn and look around as if in amazement. The angel walks out and stands behind the table where the phone was, carrying a book.)

Beth: Where are we?

Jill: Isn't this the most incredible place you have ever seen?

Beth: Jill, where are we?

Jill: Judging by those pearly gates and that angel standing over there, I'd say we were standing at the doors of heaven.

Beth: Heaven? What happened? How did we get here?

Jill: I don't remember. But wow! Isn't it beautiful?

Beth: Yes, it is very beautiful. So uh…what do we do now?

Jill: Well, I suppose you just walk right up to that angel over there, give your name, and as long as it is in that book, you pass through the gates.

Beth: Oh…and what if it's not? *(Beth gets a worried look on her face as the scene ends.)*

◆◆◆ Discussion Activity ◆◆◆

Begin by discussing whether or not the teenagers in your group believe Beth's name would have been written in the Angel's book. Be sure to have them justify their statements.

After a discussion, ask:

● How can we know or discover what real truth is?

● Is there such a thing as absolute truth—meaning a single truth which is true for all people at all times? Explain your answer.

● Some people suggest that it doesn't matter what religion we believe as long as we are good people. What do you believe?

● What difference does it make if we believe that only through Christ we can find *the way, the truth and the life?*

Read the passage from Philippians 2:9-11. Say: God promises that a day will come when everyone will bow at the name of Jesus and confess that he is Lord. Ask:

● Who is this passage speaking to?

● How does it relate to those who don't believe that Christ is the way to eternal life?

Bull's-Eye

Scripture: John 14:6

Topic: Perspectives on God

Setting: The scene takes place in the *Dating Game* studio. The set will need a bull's-eye drawn on the floor. Bob will sit in the middle of it facing the audience. The contestants will stand behind him in the largest ring of the bull's-eye, hidden from Bob's view. Each girl who matches Bob's answer will move to the next smallest ring in front of her, until one finally reaches Bob in the middle.

Props: You'll need a chair that sits in the middle of the bull's-eye; cards for the contestants to carry; and a red, blue, and yellow card for Louisa.

Characters:

Cameron Roberts—the host of the show

Bob—a surfer-looking dude that is kind of goofy. He laughs and wipes his nose with his hand a lot.

Louisa—Cameron's lovely assistant

Ty—contestant number one, exotic and New Age

Clara—contestant number two, a smart librarian type with glasses, who is an atheist

Stacy—contestant number three, blond and ditzy.

◆◆◆ Script ◆◆◆

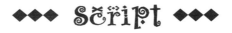

(Louisa should be standing on the side of the stage holding the three colored cards.)

Cameron: Goooood evening and welcome to this week's edition of *Bull's Eye*. The show where dating is our game. I'm Cameron Roberts, reminding you that there are no right answers, just matching ones! If you're tuning in for the first time, you'll be interested to know that our dating candidate is selected from a pool of cards and letters that we receive. Let's bring out today's "hot date." Bob, come on out!

(Bob runs out waving and mouthing "hi, mom" to the camera.)

Cameron: Hey, Bob!

(They do a funny high-five handshake sort of thing.)

Cameron: You ready for a big date?

Bob: *(With a goofy laugh)* Yeah, dude! I am ready! Bring on the babes!

Cameron: In due time, my friend, in due time. First, of course, you must choose the topic for today's questions from the colored cards that our lovely Louisa is holding. What'll it be, Bob? You want the red, the blue, or the yellow card today?

Bob: Well, Cam, I'll take the…the blue card!

Cameron: OK, Louisa, let's show Bob the topics he didn't choose first. What's on the red card?

Louisa: Cameron, the red card asks questions about the use of spandex!

Bob: *(Wipes his nose and laughs.)* Coo-ol!

Cameron: Louisa, what's on the yellow card?

Louisa: The yellow card asks questions about teddy bears.

Cameron: Do you have a teddy bear, Bob?

Bob: *(Wipes his nose again and laughs.)* Uh…yeah, dude!

Cameron: Well, Bob, it's time to learn what topic you did choose. Louisa, what's on the blue card?!

Louisa: Cameron, Bob will be asked questions today that refer to God and religious beliefs.

Cameron: You hear that, Bob? You will be asked questions today about God and other religious beliefs. You know anything about God, Bob?

Bob: A little.

Cameron: Tell us, Bob, do you believe in God?

Bob: For sure, dude. Like once I was surfing, and this granddaddy wave came along and sucked me right under, dude. Man, I wouldn't have made it if there wasn't a God somewhere out there. Like, I almost drowned!

Cameron: Real good, Bob, real good! Now you know how the game is played. I will ask you the questions from the topic you chose. Whichever girl comes closest to matching your answer wins an all-expense-paid date with you for a full evening of fun.

Bob: *(Wipes his nose and laughs.)* Coo-ol!

Cameron: OK, Bob, you take a seat here in the middle of the bull's eye while I introduce our three lovely contestants. *(Bob sits down, and the three girls walk out.)* OK, girls, say hello to Bob.

Ty: *(In a sexy voice)* Hello, Bob. *(Bob of course wipes his nose and laughs.)*

Clara: *(Businesslike)* Nice to meet you, Bob.

Stacy: *(Perky)* Like, hi, Bob!

Cameron: Bob, you have just heard from Ty *(Ty waves to audience)*, Clara *(waves)*, and Stacy.

(Stacy moves back and forth waving like a beauty queen.)

Bob: *(Wipes his nose and laughs.)* Coo-ol!

Cameron: OK, Bob, are you ready for our first question?

Bob: I'm ready, shoot!

Cameron: All right! Girls, you have already been asked these questions backstage and have written your answers on the cards in front of you. Are you ready?

(They all nod yes.)

Cameron: OK, here we go. Bob, who created the earth?

Bob: Uh...hmmm...I think it was...uh...wasn't it that Einstein dude?

Cameron: Is that your answer Bob? Einstein?

Bob: Uh...yeah!

Cameron: OK, girls, hold up your cards, and let's see if anyone agrees with Bob. Ty, tell us your answer.

Ty: The gods of nature and love.

Cameron: Fine. Clara, what is your answer?

Clara: It was not a man, but an event. My answer is the big-bang theory!

Cameron: OK, and Stacy?

Stacy: Like...I think it was...God?

Cameron: Nice answer, Stacy. But it doesn't match Bob's. In fact, Bob, it looks like none of our contestants agreed with your answer on this round. So no one moves ahead. Let's try another question. When you think of mercy, what one word comes to your mind?

Bob: Uh..."Allah."

Cameron: "Allah?" Are you Muslim?

Bob: No, dude, but some of my friends are!

Cameron: All right, girls, let's see those cards! Ty?

Ty: I put "Allah"! Many friends from my past life are Muslim too!

Cameron: Good job! Step ahead one space on the target.

(She steps to the next ring.)

Cameron: Clara, what is your answer?

Clara: My answer is "Judgment."

Cameron: "Judgment?" That's interesting! Stacy, what is your answer?

Stacy: Bob, my answer is "Mother Teresa"!

Cameron: Good answer, but it doesn't match up with Bob's. Right now, Ty is in the lead. Here we go with our next question. Where do you go when you die?

Bob: That's easy, dude, you go to that...to that piece of pie in the sky?

Cameron: Are you referring to heaven?

Bob: *(Wipes his nose and laughs.)* Yeah, dude! Heaven!

Cameron: Okey-dokey! Ty?

Ty: *(Holds up her card.)* We are reincarnated, Bob!

Cameron: No match there. Clara?

Clara: *(Holds up her card.)* Dust!

Cameron: Sorry, Clara! Stacy?

Stacy: *(Holds up her card.)* Bob, I put "heaven or hell."

Cameron: Well, Stacy, that is the answer that most closely resembles Bob's, so you move ahead one space.

(She moves ahead.)

Cameron: Bob, you only answered "heaven." Did you mean the same thing as Stacy, heaven or hell?

Bob: No, dude, I don't believe in any hell. We get enough of that on earth! When we die we gotta go to a better place. You know what I mean?

Cameron: I guess we'll all find out one day. OK, next question. If there is a heaven, how do you get there?

Bob: Well, dude, you just do a lot of good things! *(Wipes his nose and laughs.)*

Cameron: So, "good works" is your answer?

Bob: Uh…yeah, sure!

Cameron: OK, good works it is. Ty, what is your answer?

Ty: Cameron, I believe we go from this life to another, and heaven is a relative term. So I put "actions," because I think it is your actions in this life that will determine what happens to you in your next life.

Cameron: *(Pretends to talk with someone offstage.)* Judges, is that close enough? They say OK! Ty, move ahead another step! OK, Clara, you can still catch up. What is your answer?

Clara: Well, Cameron, since I don't believe in God, I don't believe in heaven or hell or any of that nonsense! But, the so-called Christians that I've met say that you must act like that man Jesus, so…for the sake of an answer, I put "Jesus."

Cameron: Sorry, Clara, that doesn't match up with Bob. Better luck next round. Stacy, what is your answer?

Stacy: Well, Cameron, uh…oh…I think…well…I think that if you're like…a girl, say, like…me *(giggles)*, you have to marry someone who will pray for you and ask God to let you in. After all, they say it's a man's world!

Cameron: Well, Stacy, that answer leaves you in second place. Next question. What…Bob, is God like?

Bob: God is like this totally coo-ol dude. He's…uh…he's like uh…say…maybe…Leonardo DiCaprio…everybody worships him!

Cameron: OK, Bob, so you say that God is like a movie star?

Bob: *(Wipes his nose and laughs.)* Yeah, that's it! Like a movie star!

Cameron: Ty, let us see your answer!

Ty: OK, Cameron. I put that God is like a feeling. We are all gods. God is a state of being that lies deep within our persona.

Cameron: Right. Clara?

Clara: *(Holds up a card.)* "Nonexistent," Cameron!

Cameron: Not what we're looking for, Clara, sorry! OK, Stacy? What do you have?

Stacy: I put that God is like a teddy bear, all warm and fuzzy!

Cameron: I'm afraid that answer would have worked better for our teddy bear category! No matches on this round. OK, last round. The contestant who matches this answer correctly gets to move up two spaces. Stacy, that means that you still have a shot at it. Who will it be, ladies and gentlemen, Ty or Stacy? You do know that if neither of you answers correctly, Bob goes home with no date! Clara, it looks like you are out of the running for a date with Bob; however, if your answer matches Bob's on this round, you will win a complimentary *Bull's-Eye* board game to take home and play with your friends! Here we go! If you had to describe God in one word to a friend, what would it be? Bob?

Bob: Uh..."Coo-ol!"

Cameron: OK, Ty, we're looking for "Coo-ol!" What is your answer?

Ty: Bob, my answer is "Spiritual." *(Holds up her last card.)*

Cameron: Not a match, sorry, Ty. Clara?

Clara: "Hoax!" *(Holds up her card.)*

Cameron: Too bad, Clara, you go home empty-handed! Stacy?

Stacy: *(Holds up card.)* Well, Cameron, when I was a little girl, my granddaddy always told me that he was the beginning and the end.

Cameron: But, Stacy, that is more than one word!

Stacy: Well, Cameron, it's hard to describe God in just one word, but if I had to choose just one, I guess I would say he is "everything!"

Cameron: That is a nice answer, Stacy, but not a match! Oh, Bob! Bob...Bob...Bob!... I'm afraid we're just going to have to send you home without a date!

Bob: Oh, man!

Cameron: Sorry! *(Shakes Bob's hand.)* We will give you a chance to meet these lovely young ladies though. Girls, you had some great answers today; I'm sorry none of them matched. Come on down here and meet Bob.

(Each one hugs Bob or shakes his hand.)

Cameron: It was nice to meet all of you! Wave goodbye to our viewing audience.

(Everyone waves.)

Cameron: Good night, and see you on our next *Bull's-Eye!*

◆◆◆ Discussion Questions ◆◆◆

After the skit, discuss the following questions:
- **Describe in your own words what you think God is really like.**
- **Why does it matter what and who you believe?**
- **Can we get to heaven without a relationship with Christ?**

Say: **There are many perspectives of God and many religions on this planet.** Ask: **What does it mean in John 14:6 when Jesus answered, "I am the way and the truth and the life. No one comes to the Father except through me"?**

Discuss various ways to respond when teenagers encounter those who believe differently than they do.

Subject Index

Scripture Index